[*sic*]

A MEMOIR

JOSHUA CODY

W. W. NORTON & COMPANY | NEW YORK · LONDON

For information about permission to reproduce selections from
this book, write to Permissions, W. W. Norton & Company, Inc.,
500 Fifth Avenue, New York, NY 10110

For information about special discounts for bulk purchases, please contact
W. W. Norton Special Sales at specialsales@wwnorton.com or 800-233-4830

Manufacturing by Courier Westford
Book design by Chris Welch
Production manager: Devon Zahn

Library of Congress Cataloging-in-Publication Data

Cody, Joshua.
[Sic] : a memoir / Joshua Cody. — 1st ed.
p. cm.
Includes bibliographical references.
ISBN 978-0-393-08106-0 (hardcover)
1. Cody, Joshua—Health. 2. Cancer—Patients—New York (State)—New York—Biography.
3. Composers—New York (State)—New York—Biography. I. Title.
RC265.6.C63 2011
362.196'9940092—dc23
[B]
2011026035

W. W. Norton & Company, Inc.
500 Fifth Avenue, New York, N.Y. 10110
www.wwnorton.com

W. W. Norton & Company Ltd.
Castle House, 75/76 Wells Street, London W1T 3QT

1 2 3 4 5 6 7 8 9 0

I. THE DIVINE PROPORTION · 1

II. ACT II · 36

III. THE SLAVE MARKET · 65

IV. THE CATALOGUE ARIA · 77

V. SISTER MORPHINE · 105

VI. WAS PICASSO SMART? · 136

VII. A SERIES OF VIGNETTES, WHICH TURN TO
MELODRAMA · 181

VIII. GUTENBERG'S FOLLY · 215

IX. THE AGE OF INNOCENCE · 248

X. CANAL STREET · 257

Acknowledgments · 261

Notes · 263

Credits · 265

The text that follows is a memoir. With the exception of members of my immediate family, I have altered the names and scenarios of all persons figured herein in order to preserve their privacy. Thank you for your understanding. We will now return to the program.

I

THE DIVINE PROPORTION

There is no excellent beauty that hath not
some strangeness in the proportion.

—*Francis Bacon*, Of Beauty

Twelve sessions, one every two weeks; but you
have no idea what this means, really, I mean how could you,
and neither does anyone else, so everybody's at a loss for
words; and it's ironically reminiscent of those lead grey–
laden, amaranthine after-school afternoons of childhood, on
the dusty playground, class is out but it's still too early to go
home, so you wait with the others, and there's no need to speak
and there's the sense of communion. The big difference is that
now, here, there is, palpably, the need to speak. Thing is
nobody can. The unspoken words, ultimately, are "What's it
going to be like?" And that'd be a funny question even if somebody could voice it: not what is it going to *be*, but what is it going
to *be like*? But anyway nobody says it out loud, so what can you

do but ignore the odors and peruse the list of side effects, around eighty per drug, ordered into three categories, common side effects, uncommon side effects, rare side effects. (Death was inevitably included, and was inevitably "rare.") They hand this information to you on orange pamphlets, professionally printed, the Garamond font levelheaded, direct but never alarming, confidential, appropriate; poised; the thickness of the paper just right, more consequential than flimsy copy stock, but a good long way from cardboard, which would be terrifyingly permanent. The care that takes, the thought that goes into it: all the parameters are really masterfully designed, as if the hospital had hired a PhD in semiotics from Brown. The rhetoric. You're dealing with a balance not easy to achieve. One of my favorite devices was what screenwriters call the plant: "You may notice . . ." It was always answered by the payoff ". . . this is temporary." "You may notice x; this is temporary." (Well, not in the case of death. They never write, "You may notice death; this is not temporary." That's understood.) I read these pamphlets over and over, like a mantra; they're trying to normalize the experience, to throw the patient back into civilization, which is where the patient was, at some point in the past—the patient realizes this, remembers being there, what it was like: what it felt like, how things tasted differently, how different kinds of fabric smelled differently, how even the air smelled differently, somehow: how watching a football game then was so different from watching one now; how different the meanings of things were then—even the meanings of things as simple as water, or taxonomy, or, indeed, what it means to mean. Once, the patient was a child wondrous at the mysterious fact, just learned, that some people are left-handed and some aren't: dividing humanity in two like that: the child wondered why he was one, not the other. Or once, it was nighttime, and the patient was a child sitting in an airport, pretending to read a magazine but in fact watching the airplanes taxi through the tarmac, flush with anticipation of his first flight. Or, for that matter, once, the patient was a child realizing that music, and for that matter sound, and for that matter what's the difference, anyway, isn't in fact immaterial, but rather the eminently material slapping of air molecules against the tympanum in the ear, thereby rendering it the only of our arts that actually involves physical contact. Or once, the patient was standing on a playground. But now the patient—standing between those pamphlets and the unknown experience that beckons, the future to which the pamphlets point—is standing somewhere very high, a vantage point from which civilization is visible, but muted, condensed into a grey mass. I thought of Philippe Petit on that taut tightrope between the Twin Towers. They tell you, for example, how long the infusion lasts: about fifty minutes. Not that experiencing those fifty minutes for the first time will be remotely like any previous experience of fifty minutes. I wanted to know the kind of chair I was going to sit in, what color? Stripes? Canvas, or plastic? What temperature would the room be? Chilly, like David Letterman's studio? Or warm, like a pub in London? Can you (are you supposed to) listen to music, are you expected to carry on a conversation with the nurse? What's the etiquette? Are you alone, doing chemo, in a room, an enclosed space? Are there people around?

You turn around and the question is answered: it turns out there are people around—at least there were for me, I don't know how it'll be for you (because you must remember that you'll go through it too, almost certainly: it's part of life in the twenty-first century). A large open room painted in rather ghastly shades of orange. At least a dozen patients at any given time. The sheer number of people was startling. Pleasant con- versation between nurses and patients, as it turned out: the ambiance is that of an airport gate, or people on the subway, or what I imagine a nail salon must be like. At first I took the complacent cheeriness as an effort on the part of the staff to mask the dread, but after a few sessions I discovered there was in fact no artifice here, nothing feigned: that it was, for them, about as earth-shattering as a trip to the dry cleaners, another chore on the list.

The extras were suspiciously well cast, suspiciously well represented in a socioeconomic sort of way: the pinkfaced, heavyset businessman (he might as well have a highball in his fifty-nine-year-old hand); the good-looking woman wearing jeans and a nice pair of sandals, doubtless with literary ambi- tions; the gay man chatting loudly on his cell phone about Ital- ian wines; the black woman in a jogging suit, with her patient husband; the Korean girl, looking spiffy in Ann Taylor, typing on her laptop. And I never saw the same person twice. These are the twenty-first century's faces of death? Pleasant. And yet there was something exceedingly grotesque about it all, as if everyone were sitting around (I hesitate to use this image, but it did come to mind repeatedly) defecating while making affable conversation. (When I was in grade school, fifth grade I think, I read about an African tribe whose members thought nothing of defecating in public but would rather be caught dead than found eating. I think that was my first introduction to cultural relativism. On an unrelated note, I don't view art as excretory.) Chemo can be infused with a simple IV to a vein in the arm, or, as in my case, they can implant a small catheter port, a small silicone disc, into the chest, which leads directly to the jugular vein. I always felt a surge of adrenaline as the nurse pierced my chest with the needle, and the energy never really subsided but melted into the effects of the steroids, the first of four bags of liquid. The steroids do much to mask the effects of the other drugs; I'd be charged up for about forty-eight hours.

So that was what it was like, I sat there for an hour and talked to the nurse and then got up and walked out and that was that. And so it would be eleven more of these sessions, one every two weeks. Six months. Time exists only in its measurement, and we can't help but measure it: even in an anechoic chamber—an echoless room, in other words a space of total silence, they have one at Harvard—even there we have our heartbeat and our respiration tapping out a countdown, as a composer once discovered, to his dismay. Time isn't a substance that flows or flies and can thus be traced: unlike space, it cannot lurk behind a map of itself. (Calendars aren't maps. Can't be.) During the six

The Allen-Bradley Clock Tower, Rockwell Automation
Headquarters, Milwaukee, Wisconsin.

months of chemotherapy, a big clock—I imagined a big, octago-
nal, four-faced clock looming over an industrial cityscape,
perhaps a tower that marked the division between the city's
north and south sides—ticked twelve times; everything else
between those ticks was suspended animation, stasis, flatness,
against which the heartbeat bravely, fruitlessly banged its
head. (Later I learned this was called depression. Luckily it
didn't take.) The twelve "treatments" (a euphemism I learned
to detest like I detest few other words, and that is saying something) as rigid as the twelve black grooves on a child's first

cheap ruler, rigid as cuneiform. I would arrive late to my appointments as often as possible, but this wasn't an attempt to assert control, to make them, my tormentors, wait for me, to "show them who's boss." That's what a shrink would say, and indeed did. What the shrink didn't understand, among very many other things, was that my habitual tardiness was the manifestation of a patently absurd hope that some sense of the organic malleability of life could extend to these rendezvous that sliced and diced my existence apart like those things on television infomercials you see at three-thirty in the morning, just twelve low monthly payments but wait there's more. In French, the word for editing a film or television show or television commercial is *montage*, putting together; the German word is *schnitt*, slicing apart. Two-week-long strips of old film, brittle, sliced apart, sutured back together, the cuts the piercings of the chest. This'll sting for a moment, she says, pushing the needle through, the frozen little venomous mouth seeking the port, into which it will empty its vomit, its poison. In other words, this was discontinuous time, a curve broken into pixels, things didn't lead to other things, they just switched, crosscut. Since there was no trail—no path, say, from my apartment to the subway to the hospital—I often had the uncanny sense that I wasn't actually present; that the setting laid out before me was a painted illusion, for without a past leading to this present moment how could I have this present moment before me?

I'm exaggerating a little bit, because counterpointing this, I'll admit, was a different time, the time of the body: the body recovering from the infusion of poison. In complete contrast to ticking-twelve-time, body-time sang its song in slow dissolves. Gradual transformations, slow washes, a slowmoving music of colors, of thick chords. The shape of these modulations was all curves, parabolas, the organic transformations of nature, the majesty of that tempo, the utter indifference of the sunset, of cloud formations, of an increase in humidity: the pace of the needle measuring barometric pressure. It would take about two days for the steroids to wear off; this would give way to the nausea that the steroids had been veiling, but the nausea was erased beautifully with these little white pills they give you now (at about a hundred bucks a pop) that magically dissolve under the tongue. The pills act fast. But in those slim intervals between the sudden decay of one pill and the onset of another, the nausea was briefly sensible, like when you're going through mountains on one of those high-speed European trains really fast and it's all blackness in the tunnel and then a woosh and your ears pop and the white noise of the train's speed is an octave higher, and it's a blur of green and brown and white right up against the window, and far behind that stands an inviolable hillside—like in one of those late medieval paintings, where you have a glimpse of landscape perfectly in focus, through the fenestration of the castle chamber wall, which is behind the girl who looks like a discarded figurine, the weird way her neck is bent as she looks at her baby, who looks older than she does.

The little glimpses of nausea had different hues as the days went by, like there was some pure form of ultimate nausea that the body refracted, prismlike, and ordered the colors on a temporal palette; or, palimpsest-like, continually erased and re-erased the current state to reveal another that had always been behind it. The whole spectacle inevitably culminated in a kind of final chorus: a mysterious throbbing pain, as if the body required one last push to purge its cells of the poison, a dark pain that began in the lower back and radiated in crippling pulses up the spine and out. (The disease itself being a pebble thrown in water, a friend who knows told me: the rippled rings radiate out, not in.) And after that, I would feel quite normal; this usually occurred a day or two before the next chemo, chemo number x plus one. Or $12 - (x + 1)$, as I tended to think of the next one, counting backward, or calculating the percentage, or ratio: one out of twelve, two out of twelve; or two down, ten to go; three down, nine to go; four to eight; five to seven—kind of like the way they express Supreme Court decisions except there'd be twelve justices instead of however many there actually are, a figure that eleven out of twelve Americans, I'm sure, don't know.

Before I started chemo, I went on medical leave from the university where I teach as a fellowship graduate student in music (composition of music, to be precise). I didn't know if I'd be able to teach; I didn't know whether I would "breeze through," like the high-powered lawyer the nurses always talked about who never missed a day of work; or whether I'd be more like a guy I spoke to, a writer and professor, who vomited constantly for six months. As it turned out, my case was far closer to the former than the latter; I never threw up, not once, and in retrospect I certainly could have taught that semester. (Not the following one, however.) But counting down the days and observing the body became, temporarily, a full-time vocation. I wanted to perfect the art of being a patient, I read books, took a Kundalini class—a type of yoga centered on breathing, with a heavy meditation component—and practiced, practiced, practiced imagery techniques, relaxation. I even bought some green tea and drank a box of that; I couldn't stand the taste but I kept thinking of an interview with the filmmaker Jim Jarmusch I had read in the Sunday *Times* magazine, I think, and he was drinking green tea so that helped—nobody's cooler than Jim Jarmusch. The deep breath of the day: the day inhales in the morning and exhales in the evening. Meanwhile I wasn't really feeling too bad: I wasn't losing any hair, I kept wondering if any of this was really working. They kept saying don't worry—it's cumulative, it adds up. But I felt pretty good.

And then, from this point of serenity, of composure, I lost a little bit of my mind, as the series of chemo treatments tipped forward, tipping me forward—oddly enough, right at the pyramidical, diamondsharp point of the Golden Ratio.

"What's the Golden Ratio?" you might well ask. Easy to explain. Now so the thing that studying music does for someone, I think, is it gives them a real acute sensitivity to form. At least that's what it did for me. A sensitivity to where one is in relation to a frame, which could be a physical surrounding, like where you're sitting in a Starbucks, the heat of the wall next to you as opposed to the cool open space to your right. Manhattan, being an island, is a perfect arena for such unconscious observations, like the rocky ins and outs of the Peloponnese were for the Ancient Greeks. (The Persians, like us midwesterners, were stuck with plains.) The hospital I went to, for example, is on the Upper East Side, on Sixty-Eighth Street, and its location first of all is marked by the proximity of the East River, which, even if not seen, is felt in the air—there's usually a breeze—and by the sense of a border: the city tipping into the water like it's on a slope, as if the relative lack of buildings there demonstrates it's a little dangerous to build them, like in Malibu. Often there's direct sunlight, unlike in midtown proper, where the light is so often that peculiar greenish blue because it's mainly reflected off the glass of skyscrapers. (That fact also accounts for the light's seeming polydirectionality: it's always coming from multiple sources, which creates a kind of otherworldly aura or glow.) The high-rises around the hospital are dated: they were built in the 1960s, most of them, and have corner balconies: they're built out of white brick, harkening back to the Onassian era of the Mediterranean. Less cabs, more trucks on First Avenue and York, pushing the city toward its limits and pointing beyond them. Same for the 59th Street Bridge, the least elegant, most aggressively, heavily industrial of our bridges ("our" bridges: for to live in New York, like living in any great city, is to possess it): not a joiner, but an exit. There are vacant lots, rare for Manhattan, and smokestacks, iron. You get the sense that you're at the edge of the city. These types of observations can apply not only to space but to time: you can be on the edge of a day. This all might sound stupid, or obvious, but I notice it uncannily sometimes

The 59th Street Bridge, Manhattan, 1910.

and I think, again, it comes from studying music, the way in Debussy (just to pick one) the music can be wandering along for a while and you find yourself drifting, the mind is drifting, you're almost not aware of hearing anything, perhaps you've even forgotten you were listening to music in the first place, and then all of a sudden the music does something: it asserts its presence and opens up to take you in and it feels like the pilot has moved the throttle and you feel motion again and the plane's going down now, you're definitely going down, and the sun is going down and now you can make out the Empire State Building and it's casting a little shadow like the little plastic model it must have been once, in New York, and later must have been again, in Hollywood, and unceremoniously (not!) you're back in the country you were born in and you remember the odors and the way diner coffee tastes and splashes and the color of the linoleum on the floor of the bathroom you had when you were four, and you're coming down and the plane is coming down and the century is coming down and the millennium is coming down and New York is coming down, like Paris came down and Vienna came down and Persepolis came down except the difference is that for New York you're there to witness it, and that's the arrogance and the humility of the living. And you are in this plane and you are in this life, and life will end like this plane trip will end and life will show you a little pale orange Empire State Building casting a long shadow like this plane is showing you as it lands.

So the Golden Ratio—that's the point in Debussy where you get that tipping feeling. A length, whether in space or in time (here, obviously, we mean time), is divided in two: the proportion of the smaller to the longer segment is the same as the relation of the longer segment to the whole. Algebraically the situation is expressed

$$(a + b) / a = a/b$$

where

a   b

If you've studied math you can easily solve this equation. (I guess.) It's an irrational number:

$$(1 + \sqrt{5}) / 2$$

which is pretty close to 1.618, but it's irrational so the actual number would go on and on to infinity, just as irrational people do.

Artists, sculptors, composers, architects have intuitively hit on this proportion for centuries. No one really knows why the relationship is so powerfully pleasing aesthetically, but it seems to transcend cultures, media, ages. It's embedded in the Egyptian pyramids, in Japanese woodcuts, in the Acropolis in Athens, in Islamic mosques, in paintings by Leonardo, who called it the *divina proportione*, the divine proportion.

Let's say, for example—and this is what happened to me, this was how I found out—you feel a pulled muscle in your neck after lifting weights like a good young man of Midwestern stock does, and you ignore it and then you notice it again a few weeks later and you go to a doctor who tells you it's a virus and it's sure to go away, but for some reason you have a nagging feeling about it so you go see another guy who pushes a needle into your neck and tells you it's probably just a virus but it could be a tumor but even if it is, it's probably benign, and then he goes to Barbados for a week and comes back and says, tanner, that it is in fact a tumor and it is in fact malignant, and then you go see a third doctor, but the first doctor with a mustache (for that matter, a mustache and a bow tie, as if his office were in a building of cast iron and glass, with a skylight in the ceiling and a fountain at the bottom, as if he would sing with his friends in a tavern after work), and he says you should do chemotherapy twelve times at two-week intervals. The Golden Ratio would apply thusly:

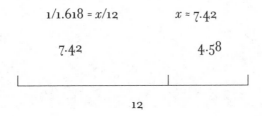

$$1/1.618 = x/12 \qquad x \approx 7.42$$

$$7.42 \qquad\qquad 4.58$$

$$12$$

Just about where it happened, just about where it tipped: the weight seems to pile up behind you like a shadow lengthening millimeter by millimeter, until it alights upon an invisible point and the scale moves level—the peak of the roller coaster: where you are, compared to where you're going, equals what you have left, compared to how much you've done. Does that make sense? For some reason it reminds me of that great scene in Steven Spielberg's masterpiece of Jewish mysticism, *Raiders of the Lost Ark*, where Indiana Jones, in Cairo and in keffiyeh— Han Solo playing T. F. Lawrence—is standing in the secret "map room" the Nazis have discovered. It's a room with a perfectly scaled three-dimensional model of ancient Cairo, very much like the three-dimensional model of Lower Manhattan I saw at Ground Zero, after September 11, showcasing the work of another Jewish mystic, Daniel Libeskind (MA, University

The Acropolis, Athens, Greece.

The Taj Mahal and the Yamuna River, Agra, India.

of Essex). Professor Jones (PhD, University of Chicago) has already explained to two government Nazi-hunters (one fat, the other thin) that the map room will divulge the hiding place of Moses's tablets inscribed with the Ten Commandments. If a prismatic medallion is stuck on the end of a staff and then fitted into a hole in the floor, a beam of sunlight, entering the chamber through a single fenestration, drawing its spotlight slowly along the room, will at a certain moment pass through the prism, focusing the sun's rays, with a baleful intensity, into a kind of laser beam that points to the hiding place of Moses's tablets. (Did Osama bin Laden, a man without a degree, have a model of my city in an underground map room?)

I had been such a model patient up until that night, the night of the Golden Ratio, and stepping out from the hospital into the river's breeze on York Avenue, I suddenly realized I was Indiana Jones disguised as an Arab, and it was time to tear off the keffiyeh (what is ethnicity, anyway, besides a keffiyeh?), throw it to the ground, and go find the Ark of the Covenant. The shadow cast by the toxicity of the chemo had reached the right length: the steroids were burning through the prism, creating a laser beam. I set out on foot, fast. No question of going home, downtown, by subway: no possibility of grabbing a cab: what was of utmost importance at this moment was the traction of concrete against my shoes, the physical movement of my deteriorating body, the aging fighter, the right hook of the disease and the left hook of treatment. What if Harrison Ford had played Jake LaMotta? George Lucas wanted somebody else for Indiana Jones: he didn't want Harrison to be seen as his "De

Niro." It was late, and the sky seemed blacker and the lights of the buildings and the cars seemed brighter than normal. I recalled reading somewhere on one of those orange pamphlets that one of the side effects of one of the drugs was "changes in vision." Everything seemed slightly crushed in, like I was viewing things through a narrow-angled lens. The city took on the magical aspect of a miniature model—tiny points of light applied with the skill and patience of some anonymous Persian artisan. New York, which I usually felt as a massive, comforting presence around me, had tightened into the knot of a Mediterranean city. The neighborhoods were flashing by: the east sixties, now the desolate east fifties, now the skyscrapers of east midtown and now—for those of you on the left side of the cabin—the sharply soft green jewel of the United Nations building, so lonely and lovely alone against the raging sea of the East River, like helpless Andromeda, ready to be sacrificed to the sea monster, chained to the rock, the Vermont marble, a rectangle of divine proportions, Stanley Kubrick's lunar monolith patiently housing the Ark of the Covenant.

And then I was in the east twenties and I went into a bar and downed a martini. That's what we do, I remember thinking: we break things up and shatter them so we can put them back together, otherwise what would we do? Because we need something to do. And the pieces don't quite fit back together, forming something new and that's called growth, like the same furniture in a new apartment. The glass of the fourth martini was a glinting lens, through which I could see for the first time what I had in fact been feeling, which might be described as

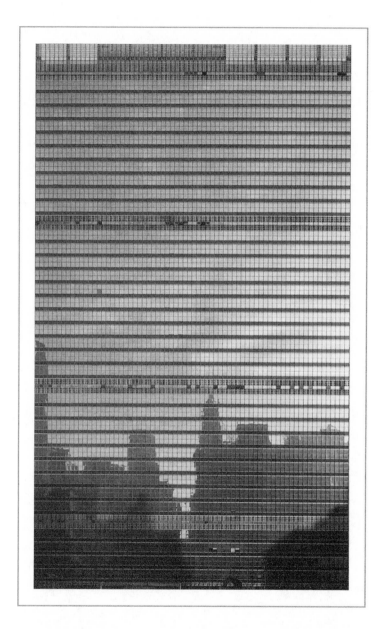

The United Nations Secretariat Building Façade, New York.

terror. But terror now was the image of a frozen explosion that could no longer cause harm and was therefore safe to view, to touch even, like a child's finger against the surprisingly velvety skin of an Egyptian cobra, safely held by its trainer; the child had been squealing in fear, partly real and partly feigned: a benefit performance for her young parents, and now the child is silent, utterly absorbed, tracing patterns on the snake-scales, gauging the differences in skin.

Children have these famously brief attention spans. I left the bar. It was chilly now. I walked through Union Square, empty, through ghosts. I was walking down the same street a relative of mine, Will Cody, had rode down on a white horse on September 4, 1884. It was a lavish parade welcoming his circus, Buffalo Bill's Wild West and Congress of Rough Riders of the World, to New York. Triumphant arches spanned the street, strewn with ribbons. Marksmen on horses; wagon trains; white scouts; Pawnee actors. The whole city watched, wearing top hats and mustaches. A five-year-old building—Madison Square Garden—housed the circus. Will would make a thrilling entrance onstage, on horseback. The spectacle ended with the destruction of an entire mining colony by a cyclone, like the one in *The Wizard of Oz*. Incredible special effects for the time: a tunnel was drilled under the Garden, through city blocks, to a state-of-the-art mechanical ventilator. When the tornado hit, the ventilator was switched on, spewing specially assembled dry leaves and newspapers into the Garden, spilling into the first few front rows of thrilled spectators. The only member of my family I knew who remembered Will was my

Aunt Edna: she had sat on his lap when she was six or seven. We all know ghosts, it's the sensation when one revisits a place one hasn't visited in a long time: my grandparents' home, a playground, a movie theater that's been converted into a restaurant. I walked past the apartment of a woman I had slept with, once, shortly after I'd moved to New York. That hadn't been that long ago. But it seemed closer to the time of Will's triumphant night. Again, the diseased are highly suspicious animals. Why was the recent past so telescoped? Because, perhaps, I was ready to die? Fight the telescoping, I told myself. Bring that night with the girl back, close. Put it closer, make it yesterday. Connect it to this moment with a hydraulic wind tunnel: let it be a bridge, not an exit: let the dry leaves and newspapers simulate the destruction of a model mining colony.

I entered my neighborhood bar. It was hot inside, moist from the kitchen and from the proximity of so many people, most of whom I know. I had been a frequent habitué; I would stop by almost every evening for a beer or two, as would many in the neighborhood. A cross section of my neighborhood, TriBeCa: older artists who'd never really made it as big as their old friends who now lived in Rome or South Africa or who had died, and had paintings at the Whitney or the Met. But these guys were doing fine, they'd bought lofts for no money at all in the early 1970s and were millionaires, at least on paper. I sat down next to a friend of mine, an employee of Con Edison, a big man, tattooed, military haircut, whose machismo was tempered by his choice of drink, a tiny glass of Dewer's and soda with a cherry. He was a devoted father of two daughters, unhappily married, who was having an affair with a bright young waitress from somewhere in Ontario, who herself was living with a high-level cocaine dealer in a luxury three-bedroom apartment on Greenwich Avenue. He dealt to the movie stars and famous musicians and sons of presidents who lived in the area, and whom we rarely saw. I was in his apartment once, when I was sleeping with the waitress's best friend. The place was spotless, and, yes, there were sugar bowls with the finest stuff I'd ever had; a luxury condo with luxury cocaine.

Our local homeless schizophrenic sat down at the bar next to me; he's a jazz aficionado who had tried, one night, to convince me that Thelonious Monk was still alive, that he'd just seen him play the night before, uptown: or rather, he didn't play. The trio—bass, drums, guitar—played a piece as a warmup and then, to applause, Monk made his thrilling entrance, as if on horseback. He sat down in front of the piano and raised his hands straight up into the air. "Like yoga!" my friend said. "Fucking nigger's doing yoga!" Monk lowered his hands toward the keyboard, a descent stretched over fifteen silent minutes, the audience rapt. His fingers, those incredible hands from which had emanated a chapter of music history, a millimeter above the keys. Then in an instant they rose slightly, slammed the lid over the keyboard with a brittle clash, and he ran offstage. The trio paused, then started another number. Monk never returned.

And here comes into the bar the restaurant crowd from the swanky establishments in the neighborhood, among the finest in the city, in their black suits, Americans, Italians, Frenchmen. Sous-chefs, managers, sommeliers, maitre d's, line cooks. All were surprised to see me. They were delighted. All of these restaurant guys were late-nighters, inveterate cokeheads. The familiar signal, no words. Not even a gesture. A look. Because the instant they discover you're an aficionado, you've gained membership in a private club, a secret society, and at the beginning the initiation fees are waived, such is the delight the senior members share at recruiting a young pledge. The meetings are held in bathrooms of bars and clubs throughout the city, and usually one must wait and listen to an entirely uninteresting monologue by the friend while he goes through the ritual of carefully (or not so carefully, depending on the level of intoxication) dumping the white powder on the shelf in front of the bathroom mirror, crushing the clumps with the pressure of a MetroCard, the old ridged wood serving as the mortar, the flimsy yellow plastic the pestle. We grind away, in titillating anticipation. Oddly, and disappointingly, these monologues often focus on politics: another tirade against the Bush doctrine, a new senator's tribulations in Albany, the pros and cons of a female in the White House, the virtues of a presidential candidate and whether he's black or white. Depending on time—there's always the added excitement of paranoia, waiting for a knock at the door—the instrument of inhalation might be the classic, tightly rolled twenty-dollar bill. Senior members of the club might carry a short, thick plastic straw with a diagonally shorn end like the forty-five-degree angle at the top of Citicorp Center on Fifty-

Third and Lexington. If time is pressing, the end of a house key transports the clump of powder to the nostril. The bathroom setting adds a nice tawdriness to the atmosphere of self-congratulation, and if it's a coed meeting, a celebratory erotic interlude is usually a foregone conclusion. The slight surge of adrenaline hits in about twenty seconds and if the powder has any degree of purity at all—which is not always the case—the clean, white thrust of pleasure is comparable to mountain air, the Rockies or even the Italian Alps. (I've never been to Nepal. Had plans to go, once.)

I felt the drug relax into the bloodstream and that little tightening up and opening at the same time, and life's pressures at last presented themselves individually, conscripted, with perfect upbringing before retiring with a bow. I thought of an old movie where the passage of time was conveyed by the pages of a daily calendar being manually pulled away. After the amount of poison I'd dumped into my body for the last few weeks, what on earth could be harmed by a half a gram of cocaine? And now it was the blissful refuge of a sudden rainstorm in the city, wherein everyone pretends to be inconvenienced, but they're secretly relieved: they're all on the phone, they look out through the office window, at the clouds, probably at about the same moment, probably looking at the same building with the diagonally shorn top. Beautiful dark blue, dark grey. Cocaine's quiet, smug euphoria. The light that brings out the truly urban hues. For the moment—demand nothing.

·

BECAUSE YOU HATE the disease, you hate yourself for having
the disease. You don't want to die: it's the opposite of suicidal;
the source of the rage and shame is in the will to live itself. You
want to annihilate your diseased self in some kind of life-
affirming self-immolation. You don't want to be the sick one.
The diseased are repulsive; you sequester yourself as the sick
were sequestered in a medieval city. But it's not suicidal. My
college roommate was suicidal. He was profoundly sad; he had
lost his mother at seven and never fully recovered from this.
He was one of the most intelligent people I'd ever known but
more than this he was curious. He was conservative, a fan of
William F. Buckley and a Reaganite, but was never judgmental.
When I say "sad," such a banal word, I think it really is perhaps
the best one, better than despairing or melancholic; he was
always in good humor, always wry. I had just flown back from
Paris—I'd been listening to Debussy on the plane, had a lay-
over in New York, the plane tipped, and we descended, and the
sun was going down, and the Empire State Building looked
orange and it cast a little shadow as we came down, then we
went up again and I landed in Chicago—and the front door to
the tiny old farmhouse we rented in Evanston was open in spite
of the cold. The television in the living room was on, and there
were two empty bottles of scotch on the floor, one standing, the
other on its side. I remember wondering when it had stopped
rolling. My landlord was standing there, with a bunch of
policemen. "So you've heard?" he said. "I can see, the way your

face looks." He'd figured I'd heard, I realized later, not because of my face, but because it was all over local TV. My roommate had finished up the two bottles of scotch sometime the previous night, left the house, and ran down Sheridan Road to the cemetery. He found a gravestone large enough to serve as a bed—a sarcophagus, really—and he took off his clothes and lay on it. His family was still trying to fly out of Denver so I had to identify the body at the morgue. It was the first time I'd seen a corpse. My roommate was somewhat disfigured by the frozen tissue but perfectly recognizable, and what was strange was not so much the traces of life in the corpse, but, retrospectively, how the traces of death, so definitive now, had been latent in the living self.

•

I SAID GOOD-BYE to everyone and left the bar and the street was cold now. Her first words—which I heard before I saw her—were (and I'm not making this up), "Hey, handsome—which way is Canal Street?"

Really? Was I still handsome? I mean if I ever was? I had just heard myself say, "Hey, beautiful. Right over there." Was she beautiful? Too dark to tell. Plus she was bundled up, a hat, a short black winter coat, a scarf around her head like a keffiyeh. She was Asian, she had a light accent: Japanese, maybe. She was small, smiling, her eyes were direct enough that her glancing around at things didn't spell nervousness, just curiosity. (As you might tell, this is perhaps the trait I value most in people.) She was looking for a bar on Canal Street, she said, to meet a friend; she wanted a drink: she hadn't had a drink all night. She'd been dancing with some other friends and had lost track of time. I've never known the thrill of closing a deal for a lot of money like my friends in finance, and I've never had the institutionally certified thrill of, say, getting into a really good law school or getting that government appointment, but this is a thrill that I know. I doubted, I told her, that her bar would still be open, since it was a few minutes after four. "You're probably right," she said. For a moment, we stood there like two schoolchildren on an empty playground. "I could use one drink, just a beer, maybe," she mused. "Is there a deli around here?"

There was, and I offered to walk her there and we smoked a cigarette together. On the way, we talked a little. I told her I was a composer and I was in the process of finishing graduate school. She was originally from Seoul and had gone to culinary school in the States and was working as a sous-chef at a restaurant in midtown. We stopped at the deli and she laughed. "I don't really want a drink anymore. But you were nice to walk me here. Let's have another cigarette and I'll walk you home." I had told her at some point that I lived in the neighborhood. We crossed lower Broadway, narrow and empty, and stood under the awning of my apartment building, a recently built, cheaply built high-rise. "It was nice to meet you," she said and smiled, and in mock courtesy I shook the slender, cool hand she had so generously ungloved, and I said I agreed it had been nice to meet. I asked her if she needed a cab.

She didn't move closer but her voice did. She admitted that what she was about to ask was going to seem absurd, and she couldn't quite believe she was going to actually ask it; she was afraid I would think her crazy, or drunk, but she wasn't. She was wondering whether I'd like to have sex with her. She said that we seemed attracted to each other, and she had a maddening desire to have sex, right now; we could just go up to your apartment, she said, and she promised that she would leave right afterward, and that we didn't even have to exchange names. "I promise you, it'll be really nice," she smiled.

"Sure, fine," I said, "I'd be delighted." I wasn't fucked up enough to not wonder if she was schizophrenic, or a prostitute, but I was fucked up enough to figure maybe the best way to answer that question was to take her upstairs. Plus I felt like I had gotten to know her fairly well over the last ten minutes, she was a good conversationalist and seemed like a nice, honest person.

We walked into my apartment and I closed the door, and it clicked behind us with a funny sound. I was suddenly self-conscious; but of course when you bring somebody over for the first time, whether a lover or a potential lover or even (or especially) just a friend, you tend to look at your own habitat through the lens of the guest's eyes. Nowhere more so, perhaps, than in New York, where one's apartment is one of the few distinguishing signals of status, where everyone is over-educated and overpaid and broke at the same time, and everyone wears basically the same clothes and has a book deal about to go through. People look at their apartments here the way people in Los Angeles look at their, and each others', cars. Of course opinions can vary widely, apartments being more complex organisms than cars, which can be translated into their cash equivalents with a simple equation, rather than a pretty complex algorithm. I remember my friend Adriane, a child-like actress, remarking, "This is what I always imagined as a grown-up's New York apartment." But an ex-girlfriend, a manicured New Jersey Italian blonde, nouveau riche, as she freely would confess, peered around with narrowed eyes as if she'd just gotten off a small plane in the middle of Africa: "Well two things are for sure, you are single, and you're not gay."

We stood there, America and Korea, facing each other, like in *High Noon*. "Take off your clothes," she ordered. At first I thought she was kidding—a little ironic jest to dispel the awkwardness everybody feels when they're about to fuck someone they've known for ten minutes. But she was serious. "No, I'm serious," she said. "Take off your clothes."

I was a little irritated. "Why don't *you* take off *your* clothes?" Ever think of *that*? How do you like it now?

"Okay," she conceded. "Why don't we both take off our clothes. One article at a time."

"Sure," I said. I took off my shirt. She crossed her arms in front of her chest and pulled her shirt up over her head, and froze there for a moment, her arms stretched up to the stars, her head wrapped in cloth: Andromeda against the rock, waiting for her sea monster: a statue of Andromeda carved out of green marble. How the Greeks could sculpt fabric! Then with a flourish, applauding the virtuosity of her body, the shirt crumpled and, released into the air, unfolded with a sigh and she looked at me modestly, amused. She was in fact beautiful. She came over and knelt before me and gently tugged down my boxers and took me in her mouth. "This is nice!" She smiled. "Half is already enough." But somehow it wasn't ridiculous.

I picked her up and carried her over to the bed, but she was aghast that I could even conceive of having intercourse without a shower first. "I have, on occasion, had sex without taking a shower immediately before," I told her.

"Europeans," she muttered, incredulous. I knew intuitively that with this epithet she was casting all non-Asians, and perhaps anyone outside of the Korean Peninsula, in the same lot, just as a Cameroonian I knew in Paris told me the word for "white folk" in one of his languages applied equally to a Pakistani as to a Finn.

The water was scalding hot; I protested and she mocked me, saying I didn't even know how to bathe. "What's this?" She had found the hard round silicone disc of the catheter that had been surgically implanted, so shallow, in my chest. "Oh, that's nothing. I'm taking medicine through that, at the hospital. It puts the medicine right into the jugular vein, so it's very clever."

"What is it—what do you have that's wrong?"

"It's no big deal," I said.

"That's good. What is it, though?"

I told her. She cried. Like anyone from the Midwest, I get alarmed when I have a life-threatening disease and I tell someone and they cry. "You don't have to cry," I said, but she

stood there frozen, abandoning her choreography, just enduring the scalding water against her cheek. The water mingled
with her tears: very New Asian cinema. That long black hair,
plastered against her marble back, matted. I held her, felt her
skeleton under her perfect skin and I felt like I was, yes, holding a bird.

"I'm sorry," she said; she embraced me, pressed her perfect
body against mine. I kissed her, for the first time—I'd been
trying to kiss her the whole time, but for some reason she
refused. I'd been wondering about this. I'd had a girlfriend in
high school who loved to have sex without kissing. One night
we had sex like this, outside, in a park (in Milwaukee), under a
structure that was briefly the tallest free-standing tower in the
world. (I'm not kidding! Milwaukee also boasts the world's
largest four-faced clock; the tower looms over a landscape of
factories and marks the division between the city's north and
south sides.) But it turned out that the Korean girl's reluctance
wasn't a fetish, she was missing an eyetooth: I'd caught her
between dentist appointments, between the extraction and the
replacement. She was self-conscious about it. I held her tight.
What could be more endearingly apocalyptic? Two war-torn
bodies silhouetted against fire.

With an elegant foot she kicked the faucet's wand and the
water was icy. I jumped, and she twirled us around twice, then
shut off the water while grabbing the four towels she had art-
fully placed just outside the shower curtain and we were
shrouded in the warmth of the fabric and of our bodies. "See
how nice it is?" she said.

She was right—it really was nice. I gave in. Europeans *are* barbarians. She seemed to accept my apology. "Now we can have sex!" she exclaimed, with peninsular, wet-rice glee. She raced across the apartment, stopped short, turned on a dime (a small, gleaming silver Mercury, not our mundane, cupronickel FDR), flashed me a glance from under a lightly etched eyebrow, and then leapt and dove into the tangled sheets on the bed like a beautiful, bright-green fly. And then it was a series of tasks, of little adventures. First we tried to scale a sheer wall; then we were flying over a miniature city, on a carpet in the air; then we dove down alongside the city's wall and all at once we were swimming together; then we were testing how long we could float on the surface, without moving; then we sank to the bottom and leapt in the underwater leaps so familiar from dreams, judging our buoyancy. Note to reader: when I was describing the proportion of the Golden Ratio I wasn't really thinking of chemo number seven, or Debussy, or the Parthenon: I was thinking of a woman's body and of her body, which was pure and ancient, and of which no part was not a beautiful surface, akin to a piece of music in which there is not a single moment that is not beautiful. That's a consistency one doesn't find too often. Or at least we don't, maybe, in the West; our music, around the time of the Renaissance, uniquely divorced itself from religion and as a consequence had to replace sustained ecstasy with dynamic contrast, meaning that beauty had to be held up against something at least slightly different in order to cue the audience, as if to say, this is beauty. And this situation—somebody onstage suddenly, apostrophically, pointing to "beauty" with a Godlike, outstretched arm, while staring directly at the naked couple (save for fig leaves) in the front row, breaking the fourth wall—this is what we mean by "drama." The anonymous seventh-century crafts-men of the sustained ecstasy of Gregorian chant wouldn't have understood any of this stuff, the creases and folds and spasms. But even nowadays you come across traces of it sometimes, that older aesthetic. Mozart, sometimes, maybe. Her body was stretched out like a tightrope strung between two towers. Of course it's entirely subjective. But then again when enough people find it in a piece by, say, Mozart, then pretty soon you're dealing with a canonized artist who is different from the real human being and then cultural critics—well, you know the rest, obviously there's no need to go on about it now.

Our fucking that night—there was obviously a ritualistic quality to it, but not in our usual sense of the word, which is a pejorative sense, artificiality, mannerisms, as when Anglo-Saxons loutishly deride the French as the "most ritualistic" of European cultures because of French table manners and the French fondness for Angkor Wat and Ancient Egypt. There's a difference between that sense of "ritualistic" and the kind of wholesale devotion to, and fervent absorption in, a certain praxis that this woman exhibited while we fucked. I hope I did too. I certainly tried. I detest the phrase "good lover" or "great lover"—"she was a marvelous lover" or "he was magnificent in bed" or "he's great in the sack"—honestly I've never even known what that means. If you love someone then you make love with them. And then being a "good lover" is like being a "good breather." But having said that, there was the sense of engaging in an experiment together, a game on which our minds and bodies were focused in synchrony, which was very conscious and very purposeful—she would talk about things— and at the same time utterly unself-conscious.

The sky was light and I was exhausted, I fell asleep and she continued quietly to do things for a while and then I fell into a deep sleep for the first time in several weeks. Some time went by. I opened my eyes at one point and noticed that she had tidied up the apartment. Moved some things around, stacked papers into neat piles, that kind of thing. "I couldn't sleep," she said. Come back to bed, I said. "Really?" she asked. Of course, I said, and she moved over and I grabbed her legs and threw her over me, over a precipice, she fell like Fay Wray falling out of the pterodactyl's winged fingers down the sheer cliff, plunging down and resurfacing with the glimpse of a bare breast. (That was 1933!) And then I asked her what her name was. "You really want to know?" Of course I did. She told me. I couldn't quite understand it, but it sounded something like Ilene, so that's how I put it in my cell phone, the cell phone that quit for good later that afternoon, ushering her, as far as I was concerned, into oblivion—there was, come to think of it, something ghostly about the whole encounter, the way she sort of materialized, like the way a girl did in a Japanese film I saw once, a black-and-white film: she floated out of mist. Or was it smoke? In black and white, mist and smoke are extraordinarily similar things; Orson Welles said the most beautiful thing in the world to film is smoke.

I'd already had a crush on my chemo nurse, a lovely, bohemian Brooklynite named (of course) Felicity, a freckled strawberry blonde with brilliant green eyes, and in typical form she had returned my affection by betraying me. Around chemo number four, I think, she'd married the father of her child, her long-term boyfriend who was incidentally (salt into the wound) the son of a prominent jazz musician. The encounter with Ilene, or whatever her name was, made the next session somewhat easier. Felicity was happy that I seemed cheerier; she wondered, I could tell, what was going on. "Still no nausea, no vomiting, no tingling in the hands and feet?" This was a rote question but there was a different inflection behind it. None of that, I told her: not even the loss of a single hair. She looked quizzical: eyes narrowed, angled, the hint of a smile.

I said, "I feel, really, pretty good—are you sure this stuff is working?"

"Oh, it's working," and now she smiled broadly, and she was wrong.

II

ACT II

At any point one may make the
division of the two hemispheres.

—*Leonardo*, Prophecies

"What's disappointing," *the man in the mustache*
and white coat and bow tie remarked, frowning at the CT scan
results, "is the area of uptake." He sat down next to me, looking
away. "With resistant cases, we usually opt for a combined treatment of radiation, a high-dose chemotherapy regime called
ICE, and a bone marrow transplant. It's relatively endurable."

The two of us were alone in the small room. Silence, like
standing on a plateau, in the wind: I wanted to go inside, but I
was already inside, in a small room. Why had I come to this
meeting—the crucial post-chemo consultation—alone? I was
tired, I suppose, of asking, asking, asking for help, for com-

panionship. Friends offer to help, and they do, but what's the cost? For they say it's free but how can it be. What a terrible realization. In other words—how's my credit in this joint, anyway? No matter the gambit, the house always wins. *È finita la cuccagna*, Mayor La Guardia might very well have said: there ain't no such thing as a free lunch, the eminent free-market economist Milton Friedman verifiably, and considerably less eloquently, did say. And TANSTAAFL, the celebrated acronym for the phrase, is anagrammatic with several phrases: my personal three favorites are "fan, at last" (speaking of Japanese black-and-white films); "fatal tans" (speaking of radiation); and "flat Satan" (speaking of certain records which, when played backward, reveal hidden messages).

But anyway I'd assumed—not irrationally—that the chemo would have worked. Because it does, in around 90 percent of cases. So why drag another friend or lover or family member to yet another wearying waiting-room wait, followed by an unemphatic, anticlimactic confirmation of the expected? Why inflict this on somebody, anybody?

Or was I just greedy: did I want the feeling of pleasure at finally hearing some good news for myself, undiluted by another's smile and relief?

But of course anyone will tell you not to go to meetings such as this one unaccompanied: if it's good news, you're stunned, and can't listen; and if it's bad news, you're stunned, and can't listen. I knew this. So maybe it was just another posture of defiance. Paul McCartney once said of John Lennon, "He's really only ever wanted to be James Dean or Marlon Brando."[1]

Although I wasn't alone, precisely; I'd brought a friend, my journal. While I had been waiting, I'd written the following. The tone is conversational, even affable; even. The penmanship flowing. Full sentences. How supremely innocent, in retrospect. Unself-conscious. Here's what we have just before the real cutoff:

> *Getting the first results of the chemo today: I sit once again under the fluorescent lights of the waiting room, flush with anxiety, discomfort—psychological discomfort. The present is uncomfortable, it has an edge to it that's thrilling in its sharpness, like wind-chill. Tired, so tired of this feeling: mind bloated from this constant dread. Life, after all, is a process, develops gradually in all its counter-rhythms, but it feels like a series of sharp edges, of sudden cuts.*
>
> *Outside the nurses make small talk, mundane conversation. Inside each room a patient sits, waiting for the door to open with a rush of air, a hiss.*
>
> *Read Updike's review of the new Jane Smiley. Updike's writing is showing wear and tear, the holes are showing through.*
>
> *Alan, the overweight guitarist from high school, so gifted. "All I do is practice guitar and masturbate. That's my entire life." Greg told me Alan had said that—he was frightened by Alan's depression.*
>
> *David Foster Wallace writing about S*

That's where the doctor came in, with the line "What's disappointing is the area of uptake" and sitting down and looking away. I wonder what I'd been about to write? "Wallace writing about S"? Who's "S"? Or what? Suicide? But I'd used a capital letter. So it's a who. Couldn't be suicide. Anyway, I didn't know the extent of Wallace's depression until after his death, and this was before that. But Wallace wrote about depression, of course. And everybody said that in retrospect his work is one long ribbon of a suicide note, but I thought it was the opposite— not the work of a depressed guy, but the work of a healthy guy who was writing about depression, compassionately. But anyway I'd used a capital letter. Sontag wrote about illness. Maybe it was "S" for Sontag? But I hadn't read her book on illness, on purpose, and I still haven't—I think I said that already, I can't remember now. And did Wallace even ever write about Sontag? If he did, I'm not aware. And if he did, and I'd read it, how could I have been aware of that fact then and not now? But I've answered my own question, obviously he might have written about Sontag somewhere, and I could have read it, and been writing about it at the point of interruption. But the only reason I offered Sontag as a possibility was that I'd been writing about my friend's depression, and the idea of illness must have been somewhere on my mind because I was sitting in a hospital room. Who's to say I wasn't changing the subject? I could have been thinking of Wallace writing about anyone whose name begins with "S"—Stefan Edberg, for example—or the title of a film or book or magazine, or the name of a country, or, obviously, any word meriting a majuscule. In any case, whatever I meant will remain forever lost at precisely that edit point, the real cutoff, the point at which that past self ceased to exist. In the past, people didn't edit films with computers like they do now, like they're doing right now, at this second; they made incisions directly on the film itself, which was laid out upon a kind of little operating table: sometimes fragments of actual film would fall on the floor, unnoticed, and then in the evening they'd be swept up by the cleaners into a dustbin, along with dirt and newspapers and dried leaves. Or sometimes footage would be collected, spooled on reels like ribbons (ribbons, after all, are what films are), locked in a room somewhere in a metal cabinet that would eventually rust, and the film stock would literally dissolve into dust. This is what happened to the film my relative Will Cody made in the fall of 1913. He turned to the new art form of "moving pictures" when he lost creative control of the live circus he'd created. He had been in debt; among other reasons, he had taken out a personal loan to cover wages for Native American performers his producers were unwilling to pay. His film, *The Indian Wars*, was a revisionist Western, envisioned as something between a narrative and a documentary. It portrayed reenactments of battles between the army and indigenous tribes as precisely as possible, at considerable cost, going back to the actual locations of the skirmishes and massacres, casting real-life veterans of the combat on both sides, rigorously following the original battle plans; Will wanted to record the past. (Oddly, this is similar to what Kubrick wanted to do for his Napoleon film; he never made it.) And then the final act dealt with Native American assimilation: pseudodocumentary footage of Indians raising hands in classrooms, or opening bank accounts, or standing in line at the art deco post office, or riveting things in a factory, or asking questions in hospital rooms. Some critics blamed this section, which they accused of didacticism, however well meaning, for the film's dismal performance at the box office.[2] ("What's disappointing is the area of uptake.") The prints of the film were nitrate, as were nearly all silent films of the silent film period, and like the vast majority of silent films—I don't think people are aware of this, the *vast* majority—*The Indian Wars* completely decomposed, along with its version of the past and along, indeed, with the past itself.

Meanwhile my oncologist was talking, in the present. I couldn't hear him. The first thing my new self realized was how strongly the room smelled of rubbing alcohol. Reeked, in fact. Overwhelming. What was the source of the odor? I glanced at the counter. All white and spotless and rectilinear, all cotton balls and white latex gloves and needles and poisons. I remember I did have the distinct impression that while I would feel a form of happiness in the future, it would be a new type of happiness profoundly unlike (and, to be honest, less happy than) any I had known. What do I mean by "happiness"? I don't mean exultant, radiant, manic joy—although there's nothing wrong with that. And I knew I would have those moments again. If I made it out of all this alive, for example. That would be exciting, ecstatic even.

What I had the sense I would miss, forever—and I think I may even have been right—are those sudden, uncued moments of inexplicable, profound, unexcited contentment. I wonder if the poet Ezra Pound—who quickly coined the term "imagism," and just as quickly, mercurial, on a dime, abandoned it—would call these moments "images," like the glimpse he had, once, of commuters on the subway in Paris, which is where I lived once—it's a city that has arcades, streets within streets, cities within cities, and buildings made of steel and glass. He saw a beautiful face within the crowd in the metro station at Place de la Concorde, which is where the guillotine stood. And then he saw another face, and another. He subsequently immortalized the whole experience in a famous poem, which you may well know, or, perhaps, remember from a class on poetry you might have taken once.

IN A STATION OF THE METRO
The apparition of these faces in the crowd;
Petals on a wet, black bough.

Like this one time I was in Düsseldorf with a couple of German friends having brunch, and it was an unseasonably warm late morning in late autumn, and we weren't saying anything of any particular importance, and nobody was in love with each other or anything like that. Just the light and the falling leaves and the sense of being safe. Or this other time when I was having my car washed in a suburb of Chicago, I was standing on the sidewalk watching, and the white sunlight—odd how much time writers spend writing about light, you'd think more of them would write more about more important things—but anyway the white sunlight fairly dashed itself against the water and the glass, jaggedly, and the attendants, these black guys clad in electric-blue scrubs wielding sponges and towels, were laughing softly and hilariously about something; and I was listening to Debussy in my head, and it was incredibly loud, and I felt, overtaking me, an enormous rush of anticipation, of the sense of potential, the impression that something vague and very good was going to happen not so long from now. It was those kinds of moments, I caught myself thinking, that would be lost to the new self.

Or this one time I was in college, driving eastward across the entire country with this woman I was in love with, and as day tipped into dusk, at the diamondsharp peak of the afternoon, we came upon the Missouri River and saw, for the first time, after hours of yellow waving grain, pitchblack steel: we crossed the bridge over the ribbon of water that bisected the country, and the landscape was orangelit, and the bridge, casting a long shadow, was pointing somewhere.

Ah, but you're saying—this could just be the old stupid romantic view of lost youth. And true, I'm part Irish, very sentimental; I remember this one time I was in the park and my then-girlfriend looked up from reading Yeats and exclaimed—all he does is talk about faded youth! My friend Sarah, also a writer (I mean, she *is* a writer—I'm not really a writer, I'm just writing this one thing and that's it), grew up in London. Every Sunday morning her father would take her to this fancy pub in the neighborhood, and they'd have coffee and read the newspaper together, and the sunlight (light again!) streaming through the windows and—well she described it better than I ever could, but at the end of her description she said, "How could I have known, then, how wonderful that was?"

My oncologist was looking at me now. Hard to read his face. I suddenly recalled that at our first consultation, he told me that he had been born in Milwaukee. Frank Lloyd Wright and Orson Welles, whom an Italian friend of mine calls the two greatest artists of the twentieth century, were both born near Milwaukee. I was born in Milwaukee too. My parents were very fond of the arts, although they weren't professional artists. My mom was gifted musically, and my father was gifted writerly-ly. We lived in a comfortable, Tudor-style house in a subdivision that originally, in the nineteenth century, was a grain farm for a brewery downtown founded by a German immigrant, Jacob Best. His son-in-law, Frederick Pabst, took it over and expanded the business into a very successful company: one of the company's brands, Pabst Blue Ribbon, became very popular indeed: in the 1986 movie *Blue Velvet*, a character played by Dennis Hopper talks about it even. In a 1997 book David Foster Wallace talks about this even. Eventually the brewery didn't need the farm anymore, so the farm was converted, for the burgeoning bourgeoisie, into our subdivision. The curvy streets were designed to form the shape of a Prussian military helmet. You can see this clearly from the airplane if you're flying in a south-westerly direction to Mitchell Field and if you know where to look. I love traveling and in the hospital room I realized I probably wouldn't be traveling anywhere for quite some time now. The house across the street was the original farmhouse, and our house was the second or third built, I think. They put a plaque on it, the national registry of historic buildings or whatever. The main thing in our dark orange living room was an immense old dictionary on a podium like a Torah on a bimah. It wasn't an unusual thing for my dad to amble with some urgency into the living room to look up a word; this was normal, actually. I thought all businessmen did this; but then I thought all businessmen went to work in an office building that was converted from a Victorian arcade: a building of cast iron and glass (cast iron being easier to weld than steel) with a skylight, dizzying balconies, and a fountain at the bottom: a building that not too long ago housed a billiard parlor, Turkish baths, and a bar: a city within a city. But when I was a child I didn't like the arts because I found them imprecise and meaningless. Music, above all. Couldn't stand music. I could read it and play it but I couldn't really stand it: I liked math and science, especially biology; I was a little obsessed with taxonomy. When I was in grade school, I wanted to be an ornithologist. I would try to memorize the Latin names of the birds, even though I hadn't studied Latin. This came in handy later, in high school, when I did study Latin because I had discovered girls and suddenly I had understood why people liked the arts, and science and math flew out the skylight like birds; and at the same time my father had a nervous breakdown and rediscovered literature and quit his job to write, and my parents divorced. My father told me about Ezra Pound. How Pound's grandfather had been the governor of Wisconsin. How at the age of fifteen Pound had said that by the age of thirty he would know more about poetry than any man alive, and by the age of thirty he did. When my father told me that, I was at that age where you're going across a bridge, in a sense, and whatever you read and whatever you hear will mark you forever, like it or not, and so I happened to read Pound and Eliot and Auden, and that's why I think about them all the time even though they're not fashionable; I'll probably refer to them again during this essay and I'm a little embarrassed about that; I'm afraid you'll think I'm not fashionable. Writers hope readers will like them, just like people hope other people they haven't met yet will like them. And sometimes, for this precise reason, people and artists will put up defenses, and this is why, partly, Auden called one of his great books *The Shield of Achilles*. A young woman by the name of Rachel Wetzsteon wrote a great book about Auden. The idea of a shield, and hoping people you haven't met would like you—these ideas have something to do with Rachel, I think. My father met Auden once, and he said that Auden was too shy and awkward to speak or even meet his gaze. I finished high school and went to college in Chicago and studied music. One time my father, who was living out West, in the desert, drove back and we shared an apartment for a while. The novelist Jonathan Franzen came over for dinner one night, and my father said, that's just about the cagiest guy I've ever met. So it's the same thing. Greek soldiers would face each other on plains, with heavy shields strapped to their left arms for protection. I finished college and moved to Paris and worked at a place that designed carpets, and I continued to write music. My oncologist was saying something, but I was trying to put all this together. After three or four years I moved to New York and worked at a hedge fund, briefly, and then started studying music at Columbia. Then my father died; my brother Matthew and I visited a Greek island in whose center waterfalls gave way to springs; and then I came back to New York, and planes flew into buildings, and there was much dust, and smoke, and leaves of paper, and leaves, and death; and then I felt a lump in my neck that was determined to be a malignant tumor; and it was easily treatable, and the treatment didn't work; and now I'm in this room, floating, shrieking, trying to put all this together.

Pound, I propose, is the most emblematic artist of the twentieth century because he was the most ambitious, and basically single-handedly created the English with which we're speaking and writing right now; and then a war happened, and he went insane, became a fascist, and was arrested and locked in a small open cage outdoors, and in this cage he was floating and shrieking and trying to put things together. And then he was nearly penalized with capital punishment for treason; finally, he was placed in a hospital room, from which he was later released, and he moved to Venice in Italy and finally died.

And then there's that great thing the writer C. David Heymann writes about, actually meeting Pound in Venice near the end of the old man's life. Mr. Heymann walked in and there's Pound, sitting there, saying absolutely nothing. After a long period of what must have been freakishly uncomfortable silence, Pound started rhapsodizing about Eliot and Yeats and Joyce and Ginsberg and the Beatles as if he'd known this young writer, a stranger, for years.

But then the brittle-boned figure before me had once again retired behind his impenetrable shield of reticence: he said nothing. The hands continued to work away at each other, and the eyes were quiet and far away. Then the lips began to move, searching for words which would not come.

Finally: "It is sad . . . very sad to look back."[3]

C. David Heymann's book from which the preceding passage is drawn is terrific—he wrote it when he was only thirty, for heaven's sakes. How exactly he ended up becoming, as his publisher states, "the author of several acclaimed biographies, including *Poor Little Rich Girl: The Life and Legend of Barbara Hutton*; *A Woman Named Jackie: An Intimate Biography of Jacqueline Bouvier Kennedy Onassis*; *R.F.K: A Candid Biography of Robert F. Kennedy*; and *Liz: An Intimate Biography of Elizabeth Taylor*"—I have no idea. That's quite a career trajectory. And also some of these biographies have been turned into television miniseries. Not the Pound one though. Mr. Heymann is currently in the news for alleging—for the third time!—that Bobby and Jackie did what my friend Steve in college called the "bone dance" (as in, what're you up to tonight, Steve? and he'd say, well, taking this chick out to dinner and, hopefully, doing the bone dance). I thought— and later, I discovered I was mistaken—that it's Mr. Heymann's book on Pound that includes an anecdote in which somebody visits the poet, either in Venice or at the madhouse, and Pound abruptly stops a beautiful monologue on something or other and, glancing at his listener, says, "The film breaks."

"What?" I said.

"I said," my oncologist apparently continued, "do you have any questions?"

I asked him—such a nice guy—to kindly repeat everything he just said. Ever the good student, I took notes. And note the difference in style. For *this*—not the diagnosis—was the real bifurcation. Here I'd thought all along the diagnosis was the rupture. No; the proof is in the pudding, the truth is visible in the penmanship, forever altered. And how many losses of innocence have I already described, and how many more will I have to describe, recontextualizing—which is the same as minimizing—the previous ones? How many will there be? Just when you think you are out, they pull you back in. Innocence, apparently, isn't lost in a moment, like Eve biting into an apple, like a column disappearing suddenly in a cloud of dust; innocence crumbles, sometimes over centuries; it stumbles against itself, the loss ever-widening, exactly like a sequence of modulations in Beethoven (as the nineteenth-century music theorist Heinrich Schenker described—and I paraphrase—oh now we've arrived at our cadence, our musical goal, and—oh, wait, no *now* we've arrived, and—oh no sorry _now_ we've arrived, I thought it was then but it's now but so now we can—oh no jeez sorry **_now_** we've oh no sorry **_NOW_**); exactly like the stupefying orchestral circle of fifths that leads us back to the reprise of the first ("A") section of the stupefying coda to the eighth album of those English-born but actually in a way mainly really Irish musicians Pound was talking about in the hospital with Ginsberg, *Sgt. Pepper's Lonely Hearts Club Band*, a coda that occurs after the show is over, finished, it's done, hurry up please it's time, good night ladies, good night ladies, good night, good night (next to this line, in Eliot's original *Waste Land* draft, Pound, who took the "jumble of good and bad passages"[4] and made a masterpiece out of it, had written—uniquely in his annotations!— "splendid"); and it's not over, of course, it's never over, there's always an after, there's always a coda, here in the form of a terra-cotta zephyr of a C major chord (there's still plenty of good music to be written in C major, Arnold Schoenberg, of all people, once said) wafting in and lilting down to its resolution, G, pausing just long enough for John Lennon to tell us, heartbreakingly, that nothing of what we've experienced over the last thirty-five minutes—not the initial exuberance of the masquerade; not the admission that without community we cannot live; not gazing at variegated jewels of the nighttime sky, which the unblind see as a black void, and which Joyce, who went blind, correctly catechistized as "the heaventree of stars"; not the overcoming of, as Shakespeare put it, and as Pound put it later, "the capacity to do harm"; not the joy of letting meandering thoughts meander, reasonless, for the sole sake of joy; not the heartbreak of that singular moment in life when you understand you're no longer a child (for me it was crossing a steel bridge after driving through fields of yellow grain which now were orange); not the celebration of the blissful madness of the West (the circus) or the blissful sanity of the East (the flow); not the charms of the music hall; not the glimpse of a woman wearing a cap ("a fellow will remember a lot of things you wouldn't think he'd remember," the now elderly Bernstein warns the ambitious young newsman; "she didn't see me at all, but I'll bet a month hasn't gone by since that I haven't thought of that girl"); not the rage against the machine of Madison Avenue and daytime television; not the ecstasy of the symmetry of the musical reprise (a joy unknown, until this moment, to the pop/rock album)—none of this matters, Lennon tells us, because he's just read the newspaper and—oh, boy. And now we're in minor. And we may never get out. But of course we will, unforgettably, with the help of ten hands on three pianos—one lent, uniquely, by Daniel Barenboim, just when you think the guy's exhausted pretty much any further possibility of cultural generosity, you learn something like this about him—and with the help of one of the, well, no, I'll just go ahead and say it, *the* greatest E major chord in the history of Western music,* a conclusion that

---

* Although it must be noted that E major, with its prickly four sharps, is a key seldom used by European composers of the "common practice" period, i.e., that part of musical history that encompasses what we usually call the Baroque, Classical, and Romantic periods, wherein mainstream composers are writing with major and minor scales, for specific instruments (i.e., the orchestra, the string quartet, the piano) rather than for voices with or without accompanying instruments, and rather than writing with a whole plethora of different kinds of scales that we've since lost. There is no major symphony or concerto in E major by Mozart, Beethoven, Schumann, or Brahms, and just one (a symphony) by Schubert. Mahler's Fourth Symphony ends in E major, but it doesn't start there; Mahler was a composer who dismantled the notion of the key as a unifying principle. However, in qualifying the final chord of *Sgt. Pepper's Lonely Hearts Club Band* as the greatest E major chord in European history, I may have indulged in a freefall of irrational exuberance, because Beethoven's thirtieth piano sonata is in this key. But then again, I may not have.

very nearly had been a bunch of white guys humming Tibetan chant, which incidentally is as good an illustration of the fragility of great art as the image of a forty-nine-year-old Ryan O'Neal (Paramount's original choice, to Mr. Coppola's horror—hey, the suits told him, Italians can have blond hair too) saying, "Just when I thought I was out, they pull me back in." Which would have been even worse. But we know now, in hindsight, it ends with that chord and, as the groove proves, we will never see it any other way; but before, when it was actually happening, we simply weren't sure how it would turn out.

It's also exactly like yet another fresh spring after yet another waterfall in the center of a Greek island: yet another giving away.

What I wrote now, in foreverafter altered penmanship:

> *Lymph node shrunk and is stable—not unusual*
> *Still some PET activity, much less than before*
> > *This is troubling b/c it correlates*
> *False positive rate 20/40%*
> *Money is in the chest.*
> *Media stanoscopy.*
> > *If there is persistent disease, we still have an excellent*
> *chance of getting rid of it.*
> *Autologous st*
> > *Supportive*
> *Stem cells. After chemo,*
> > *Cell separator, takes blood out, centrifuges it, get the*
> *stem cells.*

Then high dose chemo with radiation

    with autologous stem cells, back in for a transfusion,

after

      2/3 weeks, they start growing back.

Risk not huge, been doing it for 20 years.

    Mortality under 5%.

ICE. Two cycles to start with. In hospital.

    2/3 weeks, 6/9 weeks   I is continuous infusion

                         1 to 2 days

                         then more

   a little more intensive but still conventional

2) replace the port—this is the catheter

3) stem cell separator. Few days.

4) High dose chemo with radiation. 48 to 72 hrs after chemo

                    stem cells go back in.

                    Then in hospital for weeks.

Could be worse.

Pretty well tolerated.

Some risk, not too much.

Notice something? The writing's way better. Like having Pound around, but for free, without having to put up with his fascism. (Joyce was "genuinely frightened of him" and wouldn't meet him for dinner in Paris in 1934 if Hemingway wouldn't come along.)[5]

Then I said, how long will all this take?

"A year."

Okay and we shook hands and I walked outside and kept walking and when I reached Park Avenue I called a friend of mine with whom I'd been speaking during the six months of chemo; she'd had the same thing, she'd done the same chemo and was fine. I told her that for me there was some "uptake" on the scan results and that I was going to have a bone marrow transplant, and she started sobbing uncontrollably, crying, "But that can't be true, that's not true. That's salvage treatment, you're not going to die. You have to go to another hospital, because that can't be true." Now this reaction made me feel a little uneasy, like Eurydice must have felt when she saw the look on her boyfriend's face ahead of her, and felt herself slipping into Hades. I called my friend Carmilla. She told me where to meet her, a pan-Asian restaurant in Chelsea. I jumped in a cab and watched the old Pan Am Building, now the MetLife Building, swell.

She was at the bar with about a dozen plates of dim sum in front of her. She hugged me tightly and gave me a deep kiss, then handed me a martini; and the second act began.

·

SHE HUGGED ME tightly and gave me a deep kiss, then handed me a martini—freeze it there for a sec. This should not be taken as a value judgment, but just as lives may be thus bisected, so doth humanity divide itself, for some inscrutable reason, between people who seem illuminated from above, and those who seem lit from below. (I mean "seem illuminated" *literally*, like with light gear you see on film sets.) Either quality is no particular indicator of either intelligence (although a case could be made for a statistical correlation between intelligence and the former) or beauty (same for the latter), and anyway—thankfully—beauty and intelligence are unmasked as the combatants they truly are only upon reaching their very extremes. The above-lit slash below-lit continuum is, like virtually every other orientation (whether political, sexual, ethnic, religious, technocratic, melodic, whatever) (televised, aquatic, whatever), exactly that: a spectrum, on which the vast majority of us will fall somewhere in the middle, more or less. But God bless America. Gimme your tired, your poor. I became tired, and poor, due to treatments for a disease, and due to a disease, that had everything to do with genes and nothing to do with the environment. ("If anything," my bow-tied oncologist said once, "you could suggest a socioeconomic bias," and he smirked. That was the point where we really bonded. Even more than when he said I could keep smoking. "Quit after. Don't worry about it now. One thing at a time. Do that next." Or when I asked him about diet, herbal supplements, red cabbage, flavenoid-rich kale, antioxidants, sulfuric garlic. "Yeah, that stuff is just terrific, the whole idea's great, the only thing is that it makes absolutely no difference and it doesn't work. Listen, don't eat any of that crap. Okay?")

But back to Carmilla, sitting at the glass bar at the restaurant in Chelsea, smiling her perfect smile and kissing me and handing me a martini that gleamed: then another, and then— quite predatorily, in a way; both overflowing with kindness and embedded in herself at the same time—grabbed my wrist with her lovely hand and gave me the first real kiss. Oh and speaking of bars and restaurants, any club or bar or restaurant owner will tell you that the two most important factors for success in their field in America are (1) music and (2) lighting. The music should not be subtle, but the lighting may be subtle, hidden, even, in a warm coven: perhaps a lightweight, easily installed, energy-efficient LED strip, recessed along the edge of the bar to produce elegantly dramatic effects. Take, for example, a person whose above-lit/below-lit quotient (a^{lit}/b_{lit}) is just slightly, and to the untrained eye unnoticeably, "south" (i.e., low) of the apex $X = 1$ of the standard normal distribution curve—that is, just to the left of the tip of the top of the pear or the bump $(a^{lit}/b_{lit} < X)$. Place this person—who in the banal light of day is so normally, neutrally, unassumingly attractive— place him (or her) at the bar and what happens? Genes and environment will mix like memory and desire, slightly accentuating the inherent, latent below-lit factor that, when paired with the perfect musical accompaniment, should produce the desired effect for patron and proprietor alike: just a hint of darkened, enlarged eyes, the gentle emphasis of the cheekbones that cast shadows that trail upward. It's a win-win.

And so what of the person for whom

$$a^{lit}/b_{lit} > X$$

holds? The opposite case. This won't be on the final, you don't have to take it down, but if the bar owner is any good, then this person's natural propensity to illumination from above will be gently, safely, environmentally nudged toward the center, just as the universe itself moves irresistibly toward equilibrium, forever creating an Apollo for the Dionysus already at the bar, sipping his drink; a McCartney for a Lennon, a Pound for an Eliot; a Figaro for the Don; an Eliot for a Pound; a Rolling Stones (who merely pretended to be fucked up) for a Beatles (who were more fucked up than the world will ever, ever know): the slightly below-lit slightly exalted, the slightly above-lit gently redeemed.

But I know what you're wondering. What about Carmilla? How does someone not just slightly exalted, but for whom

$$a^{lit}/b_{lit}$$

dangerously, in natural light, veers toward the zero limit, fit into this equation? Explosively?

I haven't described her yet, but you've probably already guessed. What happens when you're dealing with somebody of such striking physical beauty that even the most intemperate climes—the Siberian fluorescence of a subway on Wednesday morning, 3 A.M.; the unforgiving Laplandic glare of a twenty-four-hour deli's illuminated Marlboro panel—are rendered perfectly helpless, breathless, catalepsic? For in Gladwellian terms, Carmilla would be an "outlier"—just like Bill Gates, the four Beatles (including Ringo and excluding George Martin, who spent less time in Hamburg), and 3,879,000,000 Asians. How will the attributes of the specimen in question—the alabaster complexion; the gentle slope of the cheeks, impossible to not caress; the, frankly, nearly charnel gaze, blissfully and indisputably countered at the last possible moment by the cyclamen lips; the shock of the crop of the inkspill of her hair

(I could have just said she was a model, but this is a little bit how my mind works when I've done a little cocaine)—how do these qualities reply to the reactive agents of that low-voltage LED strip tucked coyly behind the soda guns, beer mats, stirrers and swizzle sticks, not unlike a Cupidon hiding his eyes behind his wing? Seeing her perched upon the burnished designer barstool like a longtailed goldencheeked warbler on a wire, one can't help but wonder: will that slight draft of the recessed, beauty-infusing light simply tip her over the edge? Will it push Beauty into its close cousin, the Monstrous? Will the felicity of her Nabokovian exquisiteness finally flinch once and forever, like Eurydice slipping away—despite the lyre, the frantic fretwork, and the song—past Rushdiestan, sliding irretrievably into Lower Pynchonia?

Oddly, no. For reasons still obscure to scientists, Carmilla's status as a beacon was only heightened; she positively gleamed. Researchers can't explain it yet, but they have observed that she's endowed with the capacity to absorb virtually any source of light, partially digest it, and then (metaphorically, of course) regurgitate it, transformed, for the benefit of those mortals surrounding her who are, of course, unable to directly assimilate the light themselves. This is, after all, the ultimate expression of an exotic bird's love: softened, liquefied, partially dissolved, the light emanates through her as if it had, in fact, originated somewhere deep within her very being—like Lakshmi, the Hindu goddess of light, the embodiment of feminine beauty, and, when Rushdieless, the host of a reality show about food. This is one reason (three?) why when you're with Carmilla in a restaurant, it's not unusual for the waiters and kitchen staff and owners and clientele to form an informal circle around you and almost dance, almost like a Bollywood chorus actually dancing around Aishwarya Rai.

Carmilla and I kissed, and had a sip of our martinis, and then kissed, and then had a sip of our martinis, and kissed, and sipped our martinis. "So tell me what happened?" How low, her voice—never ceased to surprise me, a Lauren Bacall thing, Demi Moore doing—imagine!—Mamet instead of Ashton.

I told her how the six months of chemotherapy hadn't worked, how it looked as if I were moving straight into a bone marrow transplant, salvage treatment.

"You're worried about the pain."

No, I said. I'm worried about mortality: the chance of death, something unforgettably described by a woman with whom I was once in love as, simply, "the worst thing in the world": the real chance of death, not only from the transplant itself, because there was, too, the very real possibility that my disease was in fact a resistant case that would prove unresponsive even to said treatment.

"You're worried about death?" Carmilla asked me, her voice suddenly as if in the darkness, in her bedroom, as if we'd somehow just for a second flash forwarded three hours.

Yes, I said.

"Why?"

Because, I said, I don't want to die.

"Why not?" She frowned and with her face formed a ques-

59

tion mark: the stroke a raised eyebrow, the dot a shrimp dump-
ling popped in her scarlet mouth.

•

HER APARTMENT, NEXT door, was beautiful: hardwood floors
as far as the contact lens–less eye could see, and that was my
view, having removed my contacts, nearsighted, staring at her
breasts, which seemed afar. What are perfect breasts? (These.)
Times change, as Cole Porter and Eliot and the Byrds and those
guys who wrote the Bible knew so well. And then there are the
champagne glasses modeled, supposedly, to Marie Antoinette's
chest: a headless chest at the Place de la Concorde: glasses from
which we'd been drinking good champagne. And then the perfect curves of her sterling silver art deco ashtray (New York is,
after all, the essential art deco town). And this gorgeous exotic
thing, variegated now in the safe shade of her sylvan habitat,
this austere, infinitely beautiful, infinitely suffering thing
stretched out upon me, the tendons of her hamstrings taut: she
caught me staring at her perfect breasts, and—

But "perfect," after all, if I'm to use the word, must meet some
strict criteria, even universal criteria, in spite of the unceasing
capriciousness of Time: there is surely some ancient correspondence to a divine proportion between the slope, say, of the distribution curve and the diamondsharp tip of the top of the pear.

And so she caught me, glancing at her breasts—the plaster
cast of her breasts mounted on the wall like the trophy of a
hunter, or the marble fragment of a torso sculpted somewhere

thousands of miles away and thousands of years ago, once whole, once standing in shade or in sunlight, casting a shadow. And of course she didn't mind that I was gazing at her breasts, how could she have minded, that's the whole reason she'd had them cast and mounted in the first place, when they told her the double mastectomy was her sole option for survival. And that after—what? Here her story mingles in my mind with so many other similar testimonials, a tumor discovered somewhere, chemo, success, briefly, then disappointment, the discovery of another somewhere else after a few months, then more chemo and now surgery: then another few months of reprieve, maybe, before recurrence, this time fought with localized radiation, which might make one's skin fall off, as it did mine. The loss of hair: one's long used to that by now, but for her it carried specific implications (there's only room on this planet for one bald model at a time, she'd laugh). But then again for everyone it carries implications entirely specific. And yet these narratives differ in detail, but the general thrust is the same. The radiation might work for a while before a spot is discovered on a scan. More chemo then, but a different protocol. This new protocol might not work at all, and the spot turns aggressive. More surgery, then, and full-body radiation. Here the phrase "six months" might be uttered for the first time and not heard and uttered again. More chemo then, but yet another protocol. These stories, legion. This protocol, on the other hand, might seem to be working, until another "six months" is pronounced— and meanwhile you might be looking down from the window of your apartment, watching civilization wander about. And then another six months, although this time the phrase doesn't sound like it's in quotes. And maybe now, like in the tale of the martyrdom of Saint Agatha of Sicily (Carmilla considered herself half Sicilian in spite of the fact that she was merely [and merrily] a Jewish girl who had merely been married to a Sicilian), one had one's perfect breasts sliced off, but not before one had them cast in plaster, to hang on a wall. So Carmilla wasn't irritated by my admiration. On the contrary, she was flattered. In this way, her breasts still belonged to her. In this way, she was giving them, with so much else, to me. Although my hands had a problem: where should they go? The hollows of her chest. Her dear chest, and my dear hands, meeting there. And I would never tell her this, but I felt as if my hands were gripping the eyestones of a skull. And meanwhile.

But that was why she had her clitoris pierced: such a simple thing, to refocus one's erogenous zones.

And then, at some point, which would be impossible to determine on the curve of a parabola, or on a map, we were, for the moment, finished: both satiated and done. Satiated, both; and done, done with the adolescent anxiety before death—she, seemingly, forever; me temporarily, vicariously, through her.

And she was finished with treatment—she'd refused that well before this point. After the loss of her breasts, enough was enough. People in white jackets had been removing parts of her body for years. And at a certain tipping point she simply said no. She'd just had a scan that clearly showed recurrence.

You're refusing treatment? I yelled. Cleaning up. She was putting on some music.

"I know I can do it alone. It's just the mind. More treatment

Francesco Guarino, *Sant'Agata si copre la ferita*, c. 1637.

will kill me. I'm treating myself: good food, sex, vodka and cigarettes. And like I was saying before—who cares? If I go this second I'll be fine. What's the big deal about death?"

It's what we'd been talking about before. I'd been worried about death at the restaurant, leaving the restaurant, her hand grabbing mine, entering her apartment. Now I was again.

I don't want to die, I said.

"Why not?"

I want to write a book, maybe. Maybe make a movie or two. Projects. I have this idea for a movie where—

"Projects!" she screamed. She raced back to the bed, bare feet slapping against the hardwood floor, and tackled me, laughing. "Oh, sweetheart—projects. It's the moment. There are no projects. There used to be. Something switches off, at some point. Maybe part of your humanity? I can still fall in love, but if it ends—I literally couldn't give a fuck. It's not that I'm incapable of love. I'm capable. But—something throws us off, as survivors."

I'm a survivor?

"You'll get it. You'll survive this thing, believe me. I know it. But you'll leave something behind. A part of your humanity. And in a way, you care about yourself so much more, and you care about other people, so much more, much more. But the survivors walk a different line. Like suicide. Before I thought it was this big thing. Now—and let's not talk about those who are just depressed and can be saved—but for me, suicide, it doesn't really matter. The superb freedom I have—and you will have—is that of a being who's already died. And it's so sad, that you died. I can see the sadness in your face. I know that face so well: you're dead. But in a good way! I mean, it's sad. But along with this sadness is this great freedom: you can do absolutely anything, there are no consequences, it's exactly like a lucid dream, except you never wake up."

III

THE SLAVE MARKET

Her mouth crueler than a tiger's, colder
than a snake's, and beautiful beyond a
woman's. She is the deadlier Venus incarnate:

Ἀφροδίτη: πολλ μὲν ἐν θεοισι [sic]* κούκ ἀνώνυμος Θεά

[Aphrodite: I am not a nameless Goddess,
but one truly powerful among the Gods]

from Euripides, *Hippolytus* 1–2

—*Swinburne*, Essays and Studies

Carmilla, needless to say, was a free spirit. I was really dating Caroline. I can't remember exactly when I met her—I guess it must have been sometime during the first six months of chemo. I suspect I don't recall the circumstances of our first meeting because they were unremarkable: or

---

* Swinburne got this, as he got so much else, wrong: what the spurned (and more than a little defensive) Aphrodite says at the opening of Euripides' *Hippolytus* is actually "Πολλή μεν εν βροτοίσι κουκανώνυμος, Θεά," which roughly translates as "I am a Goddess mighty and of high renown, among mortals and heaven alike." She goes on to introduce herself as "Θεά κεκλημαι Κύπρις," the "Goddess of Cyprus," from whose foamy shores she famously arose: "ουρανού έσω," "celestial Aphrodite." In other words, she's pissed.

rather they were so similar to those of so many altogether remarkable meetings I was having at that time as to be virtually indistinguishable, one from the other: indistinguishable as the sea of faces I would find myself scanning, and remarkable as the one face that would gently loosen itself from the rest, the single petal on a wet black bough. Caroline's face was one of these: "petal" isn't bad, actually, because I always imagine Pound's petals as white, as I'm sure he intended, letting the reader pump up the contrast (pull-down menu: Image—Adjust—Brightness/Contrast . . .), no need to specify color, what with the cost of words in this Imagist economy. In any case, Caroline's face was white, quite white, but not unhealthy. "Wet" isn't bad either, for her eyes shined glossily, and her mouth was wide—an exigency, we might recall, to which Ian Fleming strictly held his female characters, at the risk, I'd always thought, of boring his hero. ("The only problem with beauty," my father—who unlike me had bisexual leanings—once said, "is sameness.") What if James Bond suddenly became exasperated by the repetition and turned elsewhere for satisfaction? I'm not the first to wonder that. Of course there's a difference between being

beautiful and being pretty; pretty allows for a greater degree of heterogeneity, and Caroline was textbook pretty, by which I mean features that verge to the sharper rather than the rounder side of things, along with an indefatigable winsomeness, an essential cheer that never approached shrill. And then of course she was young, and petite. So we met at a bar and suddenly we were together and that was that. And that is what was remarkable and unremarkable about this whole period; while the six months of chemo didn't have the physical effects I'd feared—I lost a bit of hair and a bit of weight, but not much—still, it couldn't have been a beauty regimen. And yet for some reason, here I was, as they say, no question about it, getting lucky!

Caroline was a dancer with the dancer's body, tight and compact, too short for ballet but well suited for the slightly but not too ironic take on old-school burlesque shows she had come to New York to produce and perform. This trope—the kid from the provinces dancing her way into the Big Apple—was such hilariously antiquated, fairy-tale stuff that it couldn't help but be utterly charming. To make ends meet, Caroline found work as a stripper, which eventually led to an even more lucrative day job as a dominatrix at an S&M club in the East Village. Caroline was not the first stripper I'd dated, but I believe she was the first professional dominatrix I'd dated. At this point, I might as well go on the record to say that I've never been a fan of strip clubs and actually have never quite understood the idea. They make me feel acutely uncomfortable. Prostitution, while the idea is depressing, and while I've never partaken, at least makes sense: desire is consummated. But strip clubs by definition and by law forbid consummation. Sure, they get around this with the loophole of the lap dance, but the lap dance is messy, absurdly overpriced, and, at least to my mind, as unerotic, because as unintimate, as an encounter could possibly be. Other than that, in a strip club, one pays to watch, and only watch. I could understand it as a kind of live pornography, but pornography—not unlike sex, with which it's closely associated—is best when shared with a partner. And everyone knows that these high-end

Wall Street strip clubs are overwhelmingly populated, every night of the week, not by couples but by men, some single, but most in groups. It's a stereotypical macho excursion, like the steakhouse, the gym, the hunt. You and six or seven of your buddies head over to the strip club and sit around Caroline or some girl from Romania or the Ukraine and everybody gets erections. What's the point of this? And if big Biff over there gets a lap dance, everybody watches and cheers him on. Why? Why does Biff enjoy this? Is he proving to his colleagues that a beautiful unclad girl gives him an erection? And that if she rubs her clothed ass along his clothed cock he will eventually ejaculate in his pants? Why would Biff's friends need to be reminded of this fact, and to, in turn, provide to Biff and to themselves irrefutable proof of their heterosexuality? I'm always reminded of being over at a friend's house in high school. I didn't know the guy well at all. He was some sort of athlete. I have no idea, actually, why I was at his place. It was like a friend of a friend of a friend, one of those. He was watching a porno, and his legs were spread wide, and he was rubbing his erection through his pants, staring at the television. I was, to say the least, uncomfortable. Then I wondered, is my discomfort symptomatic of prudishness, homophobia, repressed homosexuality, or simply a general lack of interest, at best, in another man's penis? Bingo. I have my own to worry about. I don't have the time or energy to take on another project. (It's been noted, too, that football, that least gay of sports, consists of men watching other men dance around in tights and then crumple upon each other, tired and happy.)

Feminists criticize strip clubs for the alleged degradation of women, but in my (admittedly paltry) experience the women play very little role in the equation at all. Which of course is, in its own way, degrading; but not, I think, in the way the critics mean: they're thinking of the naked slave at auction, of Gérôme's *The Slave Market*. Of all the strippers I've ever known, in fact, none felt degraded in this sense, although more than a few were somewhat mystified, or bemused, by the fact that they were actually paid to dance around and take off their shirts. (And just hold on—I'm describing a highly circumscribed, rarefied sector of the industry: these are very high-end, exclusive clubs, with sufficient security, etc. In other words, we're not talking about Eastern Europe. That's for later.)

I didn't ask Caroline too much about her stripping experiences because (a) neither of us found it particularly interesting as a subject, (b) I was more curious about her other day job as a dominatrix, and (c) we devoted much of our time to carefully fucking, because after I got the bad news that the six months of chemo did not in fact do the trick, we both were aware that in a matter of weeks I would be entering the hospital with a slight chance of never coming out, and with the certainty that there wouldn't be much fucking for a while, coming out or not. And I say "carefully" because, like every stripper I've ever fucked, coincidence or not, she had hepatitis B, and I had to be careful of that due to my already compromised immune system, which was shortly to become more compromised before being entirely eradicated—the ultimate strip tease, further than even Caroline and the girls went. Even deep kissing can be a little dangerous, so we were careful indeed, even when, after a discussion over *caccia e pepe* on the finer points of Japanese pornography—during which this professional dominatrix savored the irony

Jean-Léon Gérôme, *The Slave Market*, 1867.

that she was personally a confirmed submissive—we fucked outside on a SoHo street, her hands gripping the cold metal pipe of scaffolding. That pressing, that pressure, the tightening of the air into one's ears, the clenching of the stomach muscles, the "let us not lose a moment"—hence on the street, in the cold, I felt the *I need it now* of the addict, the compulsive, the *satyriasic*, the manic; her arms outstretched, head thrown back, her lovely midriff rippling, her lovely ankles pinned together.

Why relate all this? On October 10, 1985, Merv Griffin, on his television talk show, asked his Wisconsinite guest Orson Welles whether he (Welles) would ever write his memoirs. Mr. Griffin confessed that he was curious about Welles's marriage to the object of his (Griffin's) youthful sexual fantasies, Rita Hayworth. Welles replied that the idea of writing a kiss-and-tell repelled him. Of course, there was always something old-fashioned about Welles; maybe he was one of those born too late; and indeed, two hours after he told Mr. Griffin he'd never do such a thing, he was dead. Paul Klee, on the other hand—one of my saving graces in the hospital was an old book on Klee, I'll talk about this later—once inscribed a painting with a list of his sexual conquests. I've been trying to find my copy of this, I know I've seen it before, I know it's in my parents' collection of art books, but I've been unable to find it. Klee, who had originally wanted to become a musician, was enamored of Mozart's opera *Don Giovanni*, the story of Don Juan. A famous recording of this opera—some will say the best, conducted by Carlo Maria Giulini—was in my parents' record collection, which I discovered as a child at about the same time I uncovered the art books. There's a celebrated scene in the opera called the "catalogue aria" in which Don Juan's valet,

Leporello, goes through a list of his master's seductions. Mozart and the Rolling Stones were the two musicians I had vastly underrated until I was actually in the hospital, and the title track of the Rolling Stones' album *Some Girls* is a type of catalogue aria. So why did Klee and Mozart and the Rolling Stones write about all this, while Welles did not? I don't know. I think one reason I'm dwelling on Caroline is to reflect on the fact that all this tumescent pleasure was squeezed between so much suffering, and that this may not be unusual. Really, if you think about it, a good editor—a real old-timer, a Hollywood pro—could just cut directly from Eve biting into that apple (slightly arching an eyebrow as she catches, with her tongue, a bubble of juice mixed with her saliva) to the final twist on the cross, the expatiation, the inevitable conclusion to sensuality's vexing irritations. A real editor might tell the director that he can skip all that Act II stuff in the middle where the hero sleeps with a few girls, and somebody tries to seduce him, and there's a car chase eventually involving a speedboat and a small airplane. Oh and he's captured at one point, and is tortured, and narrowly escapes.

The dominatrix industry works pretty much along the lines of the Italian Renaissance: there are studios, there are masters, there are apprentices. (You know, like sometimes you're at the museum looking at a painting, with unbelievable colors, of Apollo or some such deity and it's attributed not to, say, Titian, but to the "school of Titian.") Caroline was an apprentice. When one of the masters decided to give up the big city and move back out West, Caroline took her place, took her clients. Caroline, with her theatrical background, her looks, and her intellectual curiosity, was a natural. Here's the irony: while Caroline didn't mind

Titian, *The Flaying of Marsyas*, 1575–76.

stripping and actually sometimes found it enjoyable, it was the
domination gig she found degrading, and she did not attribute
this to the fact that she was naturally, as she put it, a bottom.
Stripping, in its lack of intimacy, in its status as public performance, was "real." It was anonymous, and Caroline, in an invisible and protective cage, like Wonder Woman's invisible airplane,
could dance for herself, spend some quality time with herself.

She even found it a little self-indulgent, the way some girls splurge at the spa, except stripping is more narcissistic. (On the other hand you're burning calories.) But the dominatrix/submissive routine, like the therapist/patient face-off, was direct, one-to-one, and not "real" but ritualized: and not ritualized in a good way but in a depressingly self-conscious way. Her masochistic clients were drawn from the same ilk as the strip club habitués; they weren't in themselves more pathetic but, isolated, appeared so: greyer, maybe; definitely heavier. All or nearly all (I can't remember what she said, but it might have been all) were married and all were, of course, type As, Wall Streeters, lawyers, balding, heart-attack candidates. Caroline was continually surprised at the enduring effectiveness of the same template, the unvarying rote, all the clichéd trappings, from the tried and true fetish gear, the thigh-high latex stiletto boots and the leather corset, the whip that she'd pinch delicately between her thumb and elegant forefinger, cleverly disguising her lack of enthusiasm as a supremely imperious indifference. Caroline and I discovered that we were both fans of a book called *Le lien*, a startlingly moving memoir by a beautiful twenty-one-year-old French woman, Vanessa Duriès, who was tragically killed in a car accident just months after its publication. It recounts, in unashamed, frank, and sometimes intense detail, her foray into a world of what people refer to as alternative sexuality, and there's something impressive and brave and even inspiring about it. What depressed Caroline about her dominatrix sessions, and what depressed me, too, when she described them, was that they seemed to speak to the failure of what one would assume the whole idea of "alternative" sexuality was in the first place, what the philosopher Michel Foucault talked about (occasionally overdoing it, but still): sadomasochism as the harnessing of violence; the transformation of that violence into positive energy; reclaiming the passion and the white heat, white light of sexuality, making it personal, individualizing it. Subverting it. Such, at least, were the hopes. That's what Foucault found so revelatory in San Francisco in the 1970s. But we know how that turned out. Some time later Foucault was claiming that he found sex "boring." He started writing *The History of Sexuality*, which was in fact a *critique* of the West's identification of the sexual self with the true self, and while he was writing this, he died of AIDS. Every now and then I picture Caroline hearing herself shouting to her client about how small his penis was, and hearing herself doing her best to pretend she hadn't yelled this to the same guy at the same point of the same routine for thirty sessions now; or Caroline watching herself pretend to linger over the choice of the riding crop or the cat-o'-nine-tails, all the while calculating how many dollars she was making per minute, how many cents per second, and (crack!) what this would be in ("Thank you, Mistress") pounds or ("Louder!") euros.

Didn't Freud link neurosis to tedium? Wasn't the point of sex—or any fantasy, for that matter, for we must remember that (a) sex is a fantasy and (b) fantasies may be formulated without words—an escape from codification, a break in the pattern, a surprise, as Eve must have caught her breath when she heard a serpent, without opening its mouth, speak?

The night before my hospital check-in, Caroline and I went barhopping with a couple of movie industry friends of mine from LA, and we ended up at a place downtown known for waitresses that dance atop the bar, flashing the clientele. It was pathetic; they were inept. For Caroline, it was the last straw. She jumped up on the bar and demonstrated how it's done, a little like how Donna Elvira's aria *Mi tradì quell'alma ingrata* sounds in the hands of Elisabeth Schwarzkopf on the Giulini *Don Giovanni*; and Caroline's crowd, as Schwarzkopf's crowd must have been, was silenced into, yes, submission. I gazed up at her, brimming with pride. This young, gorgeous blonde girl whirling on the bar, taking off her clothes—this was my girl! I'll bet that's how Diaghilev felt, watching his Nijinski dance to Debussy at the Théatre des Champs-Elysées.

The next morning I entered the hospital. Some time after that—I don't know when, I heard about it from a common friend, later—Caroline entered rehab. How well she'd hidden whatever she was dealing with from me. Had she been waiting for me to start the hospital stay? Had she thought that I'd had enough, as it were, on my plate, without dealing with her problems? My problems were enough for the two of us? I don't know. I wouldn't put it past her; she's smart and caring like that, and she's that self-possessed. I'd have loved to have helped her as she helped me. But I've never asked her about it; the fact that she never spoke about it was a signal, at least in my interpretation, that inquiring would have been a sort of breach of protocol. But this just shows how differently different people deal with circumstances: where they draw the chalk line around the self. And anyway I only saw her once again, much later, not too long ago in fact, and we never got into it: my impression was that she's doing fine, that wonderful smile and those slightly watery eyes.

IV

THE CATALOGUE ARIA

Events which would make a life-lasting
impression on others, pass like shadows
before me, while thoughts appear like
substances. Emotions are my events.

—*Charles Maturin*, Melmoth the Wanderer

By "entering the hospital," I mean checking in for
the weeks-long inpatient stay required for the last round of
full-body radiation, the rounds of high-dose chemo, the bone
marrow transplant, and the recovery, where your immune
system is basically that of a patient with late-stage AIDS. I'd
already been going to the hospital daily for a few weeks for out-
patient radiation sessions. But now I was "entering"; it was
check-in time. And by this time, somehow, even though I'd
just seen Caroline the previous night, I'd already met Sophie.
And there we were, sitting in the waiting room. Checking into
the hospital for a multiday stay is just like checking into a
hotel, except the hospital asks you to show up at eight in the

morning or some such ungodly hour (especially considering) and then you literally wait until four in the afternoon before you're admitted. The waiting room in which Sophie and I were sitting was empty except for a woman behind the desk and a single other person, an African-American woman who was speaking quietly on her cell phone. Behind the woman at the desk was a sign that read, "No cell phones allowed in the waiting area." I noticed the sign, looked at the woman, looked at Sophie, maniacally typing something into her laptop, and hoped that Sophie wouldn't notice the sign, but of course, over the due course of time, she did.

She looked up suddenly. "Excuse me." Nobody looked at her. Louder: "Excuse me." This time, the woman at the desk looked at her, puzzled. Now Sophie fairly screamed. "Excuse me!"

The woman speaking quietly on her cell phone—obviously speaking to a family member, maybe a patient; or maybe she herself was the patient—peered at Sophie from across the otherwise empty, otherwise silent room.

Sophie answered her gaze. "No cell phones. No cell phones here. You're not allowed to have cell phones."

The woman's speechless face said—What? Sorry?

Sophie pointed at the sign. "No cell phones allowed here. Did you see the sign? Can you read the sign? No cell phones. See? Right there. See? No, see? Right there. No cell phones. It's not allowed. Could you please go outside with your cell phone? Please?"

I whispered to Sophie that it wasn't really that big of a deal. I may as well have been whispering to her in Italian, from a street corner somewhere in Prague, in the year 1787. The woman shrugged, stepped out of the room, and continued her conversation. Sophie went back to assaulting her poor laptop, writing God knows what, and I inserted my iPod earbuds, put on *Don Giovanni*, and tried to pretend that—just temporarily, just for that moment—at least one of us didn't exist.

In the "catalogue aria" in *Don Giovanni*, Don Juan's valet breaks the news to Donna Elvira—a hysterical woman hopelessly in love with the scoundrel, her ex-lover—that she's not the only girl in Europe to have slept with his boss. Living vicariously, Leporello has kept track of the others, who number,

> *In Italy, six hundred and forty;*
> *In Germany, two hundred and thirty-one;*
> *A hundred in France; in Turkey, ninety-one;*
> *But in Spain, already one thousand and three.*
> *Among these are country girls,*
> *Servant girls, city girls,*
> *Countesses, baronesses,*
> *Marchionesses, princesses,*
> *Women of every class,*
> *Every form, every age.*

(That's my translation, from the Italian. I didn't know what the Italian word "marchesine" was, and when I looked it up I didn't know its translation, "marchioness," either: it's the female version of a marquis, like the Marquis de Sade.) That's 2,065 women—more than 10 percent of Wilt Chamberlain's celebrated repertoire. And there must be more! Leporello's just talking about the girls in Spain, France, Italy, Germany, and Turkey. Now even if we interpret the country names in the broadest sense—"Germany" to mean the Holy Roman Empire and "Turkey" to mean the Ottoman Empire, which in 1787 was about to breach Belgrade—in order to get from Germany to Turkey, Don Juan must have traversed the part of Hapsburg Austria-Hungary, including Prague, that was still autonomous. It's an interesting omission, given that *Don Giovanni* was commissioned by Prague, and it was premiered there. And let's face it: both Czech women and men must realize how totally cute Czech women are: their eyes, their cheekbones, the stuff they talk about. Killer. But no matter the number, Mozart's opera begins *after* Don Juan's last conquest, a fact that often goes unnoticed, just as I tend to forget that I never actually had sex with Sophie.

Again, why would Leporello torment Donna Elvira with this litany? To commiserate with her, in mutual envy—he, jealous of his master; she, envious of his master's conquests? The secret of James Bond's appeal is that women want him and men want to be him.

Suddenly I felt a sharp poke in my side. I paused my iPod, looked at Sophie. She was typing away. (The French verb for "to strike" is *frapper*, and I've always thought it would be a great slang word for typing, as in "Sophie didn't just type: she frapped.") She didn't look at me. Then—quick as a cricket—she glanced over and winked.

Winked.

Just as quickly, she returned to frapping.

I clicked back to my playlist because I couldn't get back into Mozart after the wink, so I put on the Rolling Stones. At first it seems like Mozart and the Rolling Stones have relatively little to do with each other, until we recall that Mozart, again, conducted the premiere of *Don Giovanni* in Prague in 1787. Four years later, he died. Six years after that, Lorenzo Da Ponte, Mozart's librettist, moved to New York, where he became the first chair of Italian at Columbia University, where I studied and taught. Forty-one years after that, in 1838, Da Ponte died, and his funeral was held at St. Patrick's Old Cathedral on Mulberry Street, exactly where, exactly 133 years later, Francis Ford Coppola shot the baptism scene of *The Godfather*; exactly where, twenty-two years after that, my then-future girlfriend's grandfather's funeral service was held; exactly where, fourteen years after that, and without my knowledge, my mother, known to me only as an atheist, was secretly praying to St. Catherine because it seemed as if I might die. Her notes, from the diary she kept while I was in the hospital, are reproduced in facsimile on the following four pages.

St Catherine of Siena
Dominican Tertiary

born Siena Italy
03/25/1347
D. Rome 04/29/1380
Visions & austerities
tended to sick esp. those w/
most repulsive diseases

always suffering terrible pain
practical wisdom
In Pisa, stigmata (invisible)
marks on hands, feet, brow (Passion
of Christ)

(invisible stigmata
w/o any outward marks
she first had visible stig
thru humility she asked they
be made invisible
prayer was answered

(Sorbonne: MD Dr Dumas,
prof of religion psychology
document 05/01/1907 +
Dr. Piere Janet - Paris,
07/1901

did'nt learn to write until
  miraculously 1377

been sailord in politics
attempt on her life June 22 1377

orig St Patrick's - @
Prince + Mott streets
        on Mulberry st
    263 mulberry st 10012
  called St. Patricks old Cathedral
    destroyed by fire 1866
    re Built + re dedicated 1868
    Oldest Cath Church in NYc

  new cathedral cornerstone
    08/15/1858 -
              1858-1878

m/F 9am-8pm
Sat 9am 1 pm
  212-226-8075
      masses mostly in Spanish
        + Chinese
    English Sat 5:30pm
    Sun   9:15 am +
              12:45 pm

Old St Patricks
Cornerstone 06/18/1809
Dedicated 05/14/1815
Sidewalls 75'
inner vault 85'
80' wide x 120 feet long

Original condition
historical Erben - 3-41 organ
blt in 1852 (Henry Erben).
still used today in liturgies
less than 12 of these organs
survive in NYC

mortuary vaults beneath
outside cemetery old graves +
            tombstones
Pierre Toussaint a Black N Yorker
born a slave in Haiti
Cause for canonization is being
Considered in Rome

- see grave stones of other
   prominent NYers

little Italy
Soho
NoHo
Chinatown

1st: Irish ⎫
     German ⎬ largely
     French ⎬ impoverished
     & Italian ⎭ Communities

Today primarily
    Italian American,
    Dominican American
    Chinese American.
original Cathedral +
was seat of Arch Diocese of
NY until 05/25/1879
upon completion of present
Cathedral of St Patrick
(50th + Fifth Ave.)
now considered a Parish

1966 one of the 1st sites to be named
    a NYC landmark by NYC
Landmarks Commission

also US Dept of Interior
    National Registry of
        Historic Landmarks

But we're getting a little ahead of ourselves, six weeks or so. Back to my iPod and Sophie's frapping. What's the connection between Mozart and the Stones? Just 139 years after Da Ponte's funeral service was held at Old St. Patrick's, the Stones, in Paris (where I lived before I moved to New York), recorded their homage to New York City: the triumphant and wholly unexpected (and therefore triumphant) comeback album, the punk-appropriating *Some Girls*, the eponymous single of which stands as Mick Jagger's own catalogue aria, a satirical portrait of a misogynist, surely not the author's own voice. He begins the song complaining that women, while professing their love, are actually attracted to his financial health. Then, in the second verse, he catalogues them. French women want jewelry. Italian girls want Lamborghinis or Lancias, Fiats or Ferraris. American girls? "Everything in the world you can possibly imagine!" It's funny. The humor here is not only due to its semantic content. There's the vocal inflection on the last line, exaggeratedly distraught. There's also the fact that the rhyme scheme isn't simply broken after five pattern-establishing stanzas; it's demolished, like the house Laurel and Hardy try to build in their 1928 short *The Finishing Touch*. So formally, this stanza is a highlight, and one can't help but be disappointed that it doesn't end the central verse. But thematically, it can't, because it's transitional. As Leporello's Don Juan—and who knows how accurate his account actually is—moves breezily from Italy to Germany to France to Turkey to Spain, Mick Jagger must move from France to Italy to America to England, where he gets stuck, and now the narrative tone is inflected. It's not that British women are acquisitive; it's that they're so straitlaced he can't bear to be on the phone with them, and indeed, at times, goes to the length of simply leaving the receiver off the hook so he can't be reached. The verse-length instrumental interlude that at this point ensues gives the listener time to reflect on this scenario, and it also expresses his silence. Maybe the singer is just remembering a particular British girlfriend with whom he was temporarily irritated. Or maybe the image of a man sitting at home, phone off the hook, paints a more alarming picture: it's an image of the recluse, the paranoiac, the suicide.

The fourth verse resumes the catalogue, this time by ethnicity, not nationality. White chicks can drive him crazy; black women are sexually insatiable, and he just doesn't "have that much jam." To me, that last word always sounds like "jazz," not "jam."* Maybe that's just because I continue to think of the ety-

---

* Similarly, I had long heard the line "Don't you know the crime rate's going up up up up *up?*" in "Shattered," *Some Girls'* final song, as "Don't you know the *prime rate*'s going up up up up *up?*" I wish it had been "prime rate." It could have been, considering the year was 1978, the very peak of the federal funds rate, and considering that Mr. Jagger attended the London School of Economics. But Mr. Jagger is referring not to inflation, but to the paranoia and vigilantism that was so emblematic of New York of the seventies; thus he's referring back to one of the album's central thematic concerns. Incidentally, I've always found it curious that the two best songs written by white people about New York—"Shattered" and Talking Heads' "The Big Country," wherein the singer, flying cross-country, peers down at "the shapes I remember from maps; the shoreline; the whitecaps; a baseball diamond" and muses "I couldn't live there if you paid me to"—not only together form the essential love/hate dialectic the city generates in each and every one of its residents, but were the final songs on albums released within five weeks of each other. (Again, I'm considering songs written by white people *about* New York; one could argue that songs like the Pogues' "Fairytale of New York," Tom Waits's "Downtown Train," Springsteen's "Incident on 57th

mology of "jazz" as "jism," which strikes me as properly sala-
cious, although this etymology has apparently been disproved.
In any event, the singer's character has now been revealed as not
only possibly depressed but possibly impotent, hiding his state
behind a curtain of clichéd racist tropes. And, presently, as
xenophobic and gynophobic at the same time (a provocative
association!), noting that one must be wary of Asian women,
whose balmy docility might cover something menacing "inside
those silky sleeves." It's a gynophobia, to be fair, rendered a bit
tongue-in-cheek via the reference (knowing or unknowing?
does it matter?) to Updike's celebrated vagina metaphor. (Nicholson Baker noted that "once the sensation of the interior of a
vagina has been compared to a ballet slipper, the sexual revolution is complete.")[6] Which of the *Rabbit* volumes did that come
from? The second, I think? That would have been 1971. And
when did Rodney Dangerfield utter his immortal line, "If it

Street," Leonard Cohen's "Chelsea Hotel No. 2," Lou Reed's "Perfect Day," or
Blondie's "In the Flesh" are songs about love, loss, and desire that are *set* in New
York; that the Clash's "Broadway," Simon and Garfunkel's "The Boxer," Elton
John's "Mona Lisas and Mad Hatters," even "Walk on the Wild Side" and the
great ones by Dylan ["Hard Times in New York Town," among so many others]
are songs more about the effect New York has on a particular character or set of
characters than about the city itself—the Bee Gees' "Stayin' Alive" even speaks
of the attempt to understand the "effect on man" of the *New York Times*—and I
would not say that about "Shattered," since the narrator is so abstracted. Then
again, one could not say that New York's presence in any of these examples is
un-incidental. And when you start thinking about the sheer number of songs
written about / set in the city—even just those written by white people, including
Irving Berlin, the Magnetic Fields, Rufus Wainwright, obviously the Ramones,
not to mention Sinatra, the Sex Pistols, Stephen Sondheim, Suzanne Vega—your
head starts spinning. Didn't somebody say that no city appears in more songs?)

weren't for pickpockets, I'd have no sex life at all"? I paused my iPod and looked up at the woman behind the desk, but my name still hadn't been called. I looked at Sophie next to me. We don't really have to spend an inordinate amount of time on Sophie—seen here in profile, and again it's not her real name but, again, it's not Not Her Real Name—for the more time we spend on Sophie, the longer it will take us to bring ourselves to address Not Her Real Name herself. In fact I even hesitate to bring Sophie into this discussion because I happen to harbor a great deal of affection and admiration for her, and I am terrified by the possibility that the inadvertent disclosure of certain details regarding Sophie—the two life-size, framed photographic portraits of Sophie that hung over her bed, for instance; or the fact, entirely subjective but irresistible, that her personal wardrobe and her apartment somehow reminded me of the fake white Christmas tree Ray Liotta brings home for the family after the 1978 Lufthansa heist portrayed in *Goodfellas*; might provoke mild amusement in the reader, partly, no doubt, because these details are hilarious, which would be wholly at odds with the literary tone I am attempting to employ. But I will speak briefly of Sophie, because the potential benefits of expressing an appreciation outweigh the risks, and because her story of addiction and recovery not only is a model of courage but places a mirror up to both my illness and my brief encounter with Not Her Real Name. As I said, I met Sophie before I had bid Caroline good-bye, not that I ever bid Caroline good-bye. Perhaps I knew that trysts such as that which I shared with Caroline are typically ephemeral. Relationships do tend to appear stamped with expiry dates: the whole is apparent in the part. So when a friend of mine asked me if I wanted to meet his single friend for lunch I said yes. It was my first and only blind date. For that matter it was I think the only date I've ever had, because I've always fallen in love or lust with friends or acquaintances. My reflections, therefore, on the dating scene in New York are based on a highly limited data pool, and my experiences have been uniformly positive. Sophie and I had lunch at a nice restaurant somewhere in TriBeCa, and our conversation seemed somehow adult, tinted with shades of wisdom, sobriety, wry knowingness, shared understandings—all elements, of course, that prohibit love. She was, as our common friend had told me, very attractive, very intelligent, an arts enthusiast; we shared basic political values. She had a freelance design career that was going well. She had a great eye for fashion, architecture; after lunch, we walked across the street to the Mizrahi boutique whose undulating ceiling was designed by a friend of mine who works for Frank Gehry. It was fun, talking about clothes, fabric, stuff I don't understand. It was one of those pleasant afternoons one never seems to have but always seems to be recalling.

The next time we saw one another was not a second date. Like acts in American life, there are no second dates. There's only a first date, either successful or unsuccessful; in the former case, the second meeting is referred to euphemistically as a second date. But one always knows, right from the start. From the part one can read the whole. The second time we saw one another was dinner, and I told her that I was sick and was about to have a bone marrow transplant and she told me of her lifelong struggle and triumph over addiction. Somehow, a pact was made, a partnership was formed: and like the merger, unlike the acquisition, liquid assets were swapped to share the risk. We fast-forwarded into mid-relationship; both parties were compliant, agreeable.

I remember not knowing how to read words, but I don't remember not knowing how to read music. Sophie doesn't remember not drinking. She drank constantly: the only moments she would ever stop—*ever*—were the moments devoted to vomiting. As soon as regurgitation was complete, she would drink. The only time alcohol wasn't going into her mouth was when vomit was coming out. She blacked out constantly, of course: waking up on trains, subways, in friends' houses, hotels, on front lawns, at her parents' place, on sidewalks. I don't like thinking of her lovely cheek against cold concrete: opening her eyes to discover the x and y axes have been switched. There were other substance abuse problems too. She had been in a couple of abusive relationships, which she never really went into. I don't know if these concerned family members or lovers or what. Curiously, in spite of all this, she had been able to lead a fairly functional social life. She avoided injury; she didn't have to work because her family was wealthy enough to support her financially, though not healthy enough to support her in any other way. She had friends, relationships. Ironically, she said, if she hadn't been drinking for the first thirty years of her life, she would have, she believes, died.

However, one day this self-medication that had been preserving her sanity turned around and almost killed her—she never explained precisely how, and I had the impression that it was simply a moment of self-apprehension, rather than some physical near-death incident, although I could well be mistaken. She went immediately to an AA meeting and never touched the stuff again. I know next to nothing about AA, and I had never encountered someone with a comparable degree of addiction. The figure of the addict is such a familiar one from mass media, films, celebrities in rehab. Sophie breathed life into those clichés, traits that were familiar and strange at the same time, like finally visiting Rome. It was literally one day at a time for her, an hour at a time, sometimes a minute or a second at a time. Her face, strikingly attractive, was tightly drawn. I've never seen anyone eat so much candy—entire bags at a sitting, the bags of candy you find at a drugstore that no one ever seems to buy. She quite literally was unable to sit still. Seeing a movie, for instance, was impossible. She would shrink down in her seat, then straighten up, then leap onto my lap, then stretch out, then hop out of her seat to buy more candy. (Granted, the film I took her to was the African director Abderrahmane Sissako's *Bamako,* not the fastest moving of screwball comedies. Sissako is a beautiful filmmaker, but a minimalist.) When we first started hanging out I wondered how she slept. Later I learned it was through considerable medication. We shared a completely contrived intimacy—to the point that she would often, before a kiss, *wink*—I know you know I know you know—which does to romance what breaking the fourth wall does to the cinematic illusion of verisimilitude. The calls to the sponsor at appointed moments, the journal keeping, the form filling, all followed with the diligence of a prayer schedule. She never commented on the religious aspects of AA, a matter of some controversy. AA has its critics. And while it certainly worked for her, there was the overzealousness of the proselytizer. As I began my multiday hospital stays, with a week or so at home in between them, I was also beginning to suffer from symptoms of anxiety derived from the trauma of not simply the diagnosis but the fact that the chemo hadn't worked; I found myself inexplicably grasped by new phobias, a clenching sense of panic on the subway, for example, or when going over a bridge. I would have the sensation that time was about to stop, or that space was on the brink of bankruptcy, or that things actually ceased to exist when they were obscured. Or that suddenly it was not three in the afternoon but four in the morning, and I was the only one in the room to realize this. Such episodes would arise out of nowhere and just as quickly disappear. Meanwhile I was also enduring episodes of blind rage, directed at no one and nothing in particular except of course a malignant universe or myself at having sinned to deserve such a penalty. It was not because Sophie and I were both pretty much thoroughly occupied with our own private manias, not because we were basically total strangers to one another, that I was unable to share my experiences with her; it was because, in the throes of them, I couldn't recognize them. She recognized but misidentified them; they were familiar to her, and they scared her. One evening, we went to dinner at the apartment of a couple of dear friends of mine. We drank freely (not Sophie, of course), there was wonderful conversation, wonderful food. In the taxi on the way home over the Brooklyn Bridge I was infused suddenly with uncontrollable fury; I slammed my fist repeatedly against the seat of the cab until my hand was bruised and my fingers were bleeding. Sophie, next to me, was terrified; she had seen this type of violence before, as the result of drink or drugs, directed toward others, toward herself. She shrieked in terror, and as soon as we got off the bridge into Manhattan, the cab driver pulled over and threw us out onto the street. She screamed that my behavior confirmed what she had long suspected: I was a serious alcoholic, a drug user. This was a perfectly understandable reaction; she was relating my conduct to the world she knew; it couldn't have occurred to her that I had drunk that night in an intuitive, clumsy attempt to counter anxiety resulting from the fear of imminent death, and it didn't occur to me, either: it took a psycho-oncologist to explain it.

Rather than leave me, however, she plunged into the project of rescuing me. I had little idea why, at the time. The stress and the high-dose chemotherapy and radiation had shut down my libido, and my mood swings were unpredictable and scary to both of us. And we didn't even really know each other. Later it occurred to me the project was necessary to her own recovery, not mine. This is not to say that she was selfish: on the contrary, it was Sophie who set up the group e-mails for updates to family and friends on my progress when I became seriously incapacitated; she dealt with transportation issues when I finally was admitted for the long stay, bringing books, clothes, until the moment she finally quit; and even when she did quit, she made sure that my mother was able to take over her duties. But she had to assume this identity, as she had to assume, consciously, and with enormous effort, her other roles: girlfriend, New Yorker, freelance designer, person walking down the street, person having breakfast, person sitting down, person engaged in conversation, person giving someone a hug. None of her actions was in the least inauthentic, but her degree of alienation from goals, actions, simple states of being—the acute, inescapable self-surveillance of the addict—resembles that rarefied ontological space of the depressive, the anxious, the ill, the poet. The two of us weren't amateurs in suffering, we were very much, by now, professionals.

•

CHEMOTHERAPY AND RADIATION are as different as night and day, pagans and Christians, Laurel and Hardy. With chemo, you *feel* the slow drip of poison overtaking your body; everything is slowness, gradations. You gradually feel awful, and then gradually better. Radiation, on the other hand, doesn't work in degrees. You feel nothing. It takes about three seconds. You feel absolutely fine, until the moment when your hair falls out, your skin burns off, you're too tired to move, you're throwing up, and this is where the pain medication comes into play. At first they give you pills, but then they have to switch you to morphine. I was afraid to start the drip, for some reason; I guess I wanted to wait until the last possible minute, so that when the pain got really bad, it would have more effect. But that's not how it works. "We're gonna start the drip now," one of the staff members ordered, "because in a month the pain will be unendurable and the drip won't do any-thing anyway." My mom recorded the conversation:

> *"If you think you hurt now, you will be in agony then." I think this to be an utterly unjust and cruel statement but I say noth-ing. The doctor ignores my presence. When he tells Joshua about the upcoming "agony," Joshua is extremely calm and replies, "Oh, really?" Inside, I am trying to control my fury.*

My mom had flown in a couple of weeks into my stay. On the plane, she sat next to none other than Luke Duke himself, the venerable Wisconsinite actor Tom Wopat, star of the beloved

1979 television series *The Dukes of Hazzard*. Why was Luke Duke flying to New York? No, he wasn't fleeing that double-dealing commissioner Boss Hogg and that forever-bungling sheriff of his, Rosco. Tom had been in Milwaukee doing a tour with a musical, and the next stop was somewhere in Africa, so he was heading home to New York for a week's respite. My mom says they had a great conversation, and I believe it. He told her he was glad to get out of Milwaukee. The audiences at the show had sucked. One night, he said, there were like a dozen people out there. Why was my mom flying to New York? he asked, and she told him.

Your son is a courageous guy, Luke Duke said. I know things will be okay. But I will keep him in my prayers.

They went back to their reading, but when the plane landed he gave my mom a sweet "good-bye" and a handshake. At baggage they were on opposite ends of the carousel. His luggage tipped onto the belt first, so he grabbed his bags, and then, to my mother's surprise, walked all the way around the carousel to her and said, "I will not forget you nor your son, Mrs. Cody."

The other day I asked my mom if she remembered walking into my hospital room for the first time, and she e-mailed me (and this must be a transcription from a journal or diary she was keeping at the time, not just a response to my query):

> He is thin, which I expected. His complexion is grey. Of course, he has no hair, no eyebrows. But, most of all, his eyes are sunken into his skull and he looks like a skeleton.
> I greet him by saying, simply, "Hi, Josh, darling." I am determined not to cry. I sit down and we nervously talk.

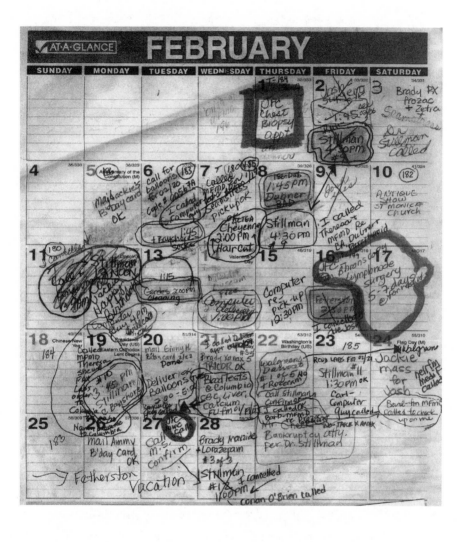

> Although I am so proud of Joshua, I feel as though my
> chest is going to explode. His manner is calm, sweet, and
> loving. He seems to appreciate that I am here.

I certainly did appreciate it. One aspect of multiday hospitalization that tends to be forgotten in the horror of it all is the
sheer complexity of performing ordinary, daily management—
mail, bills, clothes, rent, notebooks, pens, et cetera. Being
sick is very much a full-time job. Take a look at the calendar my
mom and I were keeping.

And here's a very touching page from one of my mom's notebooks that gives some sense of the constant errand-running,
the housekeeping the caretaker of the ill must sustain: running
to the local pharmacy for a certain type of soap, a certain type of
lotion; taking the subway all the way downtown to the apartment
to grab shirts, pants, Wite-Out, and Hugh Kenner's book on
Ezra Pound, *The Pound Era*, wherein Mr. Kenner states that Mr.
Pound is the most emblematic artist of the twentieth century.

What's more touching, to me, is a discussion I unfortunately
do not recall sharing with my mother regarding the question
of mariachi's assimilation of the trumpet, because that's
when they started the morphine drip.

It was also great that my mom was there when they started
the morphine drip because Sophie, who had essentially been
the unofficial chief of staff, was unfortunately forced to step
down from her position for personal reasons.

One afternoon, she came into the hospital room, and I could
immediately tell she had traded the role of Rescuer to that of I
Can No Longer Help This Man For He Will Bring Me Down.

Why/how trumpet came to
Mexico/mexican music?
Casablanca
"Bubbles"
"Chuckles"   we talked
Rick Nelson, Garden Party

Sun AM contd 2:10 AM
              05/27/07

Josh wants fm apt
Book   SOCKS
The Pound Era   briefs Boxers

Oxford Shirts Book   ATIVAN
pants   CheckBook   Ativan
          Stuff   Sunday
white out   nite for
                       sleep
            1.0 mg
            ADAVAN

Electric shaver
    no blades

Betasept soap   Kaitlin
ask fn lotion   megan
                     visited
Noxzema

        ATM   Queenies
        1278 1st Ave
        (btwn 67th + 68th

She was shaken up, trembling. Of course, she was always shaken up and on the verge of trembling. But she was awfully pale. She had just come from my apartment.

"I have something to tell you that's very difficult for me to say."

She glared at me through the corner of an eye, gauging whether I was prepared for a momentous and disturbing revelation, a horrific item that concerned not only her but me.

Note to reader: if you are ever unfortunate enough to find yourself in a close relationship with someone who has a life-threatening disease, and for whom conventional treatment has failed, and who is facing a "salvage" treatment that itself is life-threatening, DO NOT DO THIS. Because your friend will know what I knew, not imagined, feared, nor thought: Sophie had just talked to a nurse; this nurse was surprised that Sophie hadn't been informed I was going to die that afternoon.

"I was cleaning your apartment, and I found it," she said.

Found *what?* I wondered. I couldn't think of anything. A mildewed washcloth? Doubt it. Dirty laundry? Couldn't be, everything was at the cleaner's. Pornographic literature? Probably not—how would she know? It's all in French.

The glare was now bitterly accusative—I'd forced her to say it. "The cocaine."

Cocaine? I hadn't had a line of cocaine since that one night way back in October or November or whenever it was, when I hit the Golden Ratio. And I'd only ever actually had any in my apartment once. I'd never bought any. I might have had some pot laying around—a drug-dealing friend of mine had given me some for the chemo, but I never took to it. I suppose it was possible that there was a dollar bill folded into triangular eighths with some cocaine in it somewhere, an accidental residue from one of the rare points in the past when I had in my possession a dollar bill folded into triangular eighths with some cocaine in it.

No, she said, it was a whole bag. She'd found it on the bookshelf. She stared at it longingly for hours. She almost did a line. It would have sent her back straight to hell. All of her effort, all of her work against addiction, for naught, because of me. I almost killed her.

Luckily—she had no idea where she found the strength—she flushed it down the toilet. Again, I thought of *Goodfellas*: Lorraine Bracco in her bathrobe, with a firearm in her panties, flushing sixty thousand dollars' worth of powder into the sewers of Long Island.

"How much was it?" I asked Sophie. And I wanted to ask her—Did you have a firearm in your panties?

She was crying. "I just wish you the best. But I cannot be around a cocaine addict. It's too dangerous for me. I'm so sorry for you. I wish you the best, and I hope you have the strength to seek help. But I can't be that person."

Still, I felt as if I had to offer her something; I felt so guilty, having come so close to horribly murdering her. "It could have been some of that stuff Mike gave me back in October, but I really don't—"

Sophie put up a thin pale elegant wrinkled dry hand. "Stop. Please. Don't make this harder than it is." She came over to the bed, gave me a kiss on the cheek, and walked out of the hospital room and out of my life.

•

A COUPLE OF years later I saw her again. She might have
e-mailed me, or contacted me through Facebook, which I
reluctantly joined at the insistence of an unfortunate (for me)
dalliance. Or maybe we ran into each other on the street, or in
a restaurant. That might have been it. It was nice to see her.
She looked great. She had been struggling a little with her
design career, but things were looking better. I can't remember the exact circumstances, but we agreed to get together for
coffee in a couple of weeks. Lo and behold, in a couple of weeks,
she called me as I was walking downtown to Battery Park to see
a film. This time it sounded as if her teeth were clenched.

"Do you want to get a coffee?"

"Sure," I said.

"Where are you?"

Odd question. "Right now? I'm walking down to Battery
Park. Why?"

"Because I'm around the corner from your apartment. Do
you want to come back to your apartment and make coffee?"

No, I thought. I don't. "I'm on my way to see a film. I'm halfway down to Battery Park."

"What street are you on, exactly? I'm driving. I'll come meet
you."

"Okay, I'm on West Broadway and Warren—"

Our conversation was briefly interrupted by the sound of
scraping metal. "Fuck! Sorry, hang on, I just hit some asshole.
Listen, wait there, I'll be right down." She hung up. Her parents had something like thirteen Mercedes.

Given the automobile accident, she made good time. We went into a Viennese-style café; I ordered an espresso. She ordered a doppio venti nonfat mocha soy vanilla hazelnut white cinnamon thing with extra white mocha and caramel, a scissors, a roll of Scotch tape, and a Scotch tape dispenser.

"What?" said the barista.

"One doppio venti nonfat mocha soy vanilla hazelnut white cinnamon with extra white mocha and caramel, a scissors, a roll of Scotch tape, and a Scotch tape dispenser."

"You want a scissors, and Scotch tape?"

So this meeting was sort of a nice bookend to our hospital check-in, when she berated the woman on the cell phone. But just like the woman on the cell phone, the guy was compliant; maybe people treated Sophie with such sympathy because her vulnerability was so apparent, as were her brave attempts at masking it. He gave her the scissors and the tape, and she sat right down at the biggest table in the place, pulled out her massive leather portfolio, and got right to work, matting huge printouts of design prototypes. I tried making conversation, but I felt bad, interrupting her concentration. I did learn that she was going through a dry spell sales-wise, and had moved temporarily back into her parents' McMansion, the thought of which, she said, turned out to be more depressing than the actual experience, which was actually kind of fun, hanging out with them, not living alone, not constantly worrying about rent.

That's about all I learned. I sat there in silence for a time, watching her slowly cut ecru cardboard along scored lines, unwinding a strip of tape from the reel, applying it with a single bony finger.

I watched her single finger, tracing a line.

And all of a sudden, it occurred to me.

After I learned that the chemotherapy didn't work and that therefore things looked a little dimmer, but before I started up the next treatment, I had made a little, very modest feature film with some friends, because one of the things I'd always wanted to do in life—ever after having seen *Raiders of the Lost Ark* after having read an early draft of the screenplay a family friend somehow had been able to secure or steal from Lawrence Kasdan or somebody close to him (I know I said before I wasn't interested in the arts as a child but that actually wasn't true), I had memorized the screenplay and had essentially directed the film in my head, so every directorial decision, every cut or added scene, was a revelation—was to make a movie (and I would recommend it to everyone, by the way). My movie contained a scene in which a character, at a party, does lines of cocaine. We went through various mixtures of vitamin B_{12}, powdered milk, corn starch, powdered goat milk, soy baby formula, and baking soda before coming up with a simulacrum authentic even at macrolens close-ups. Packed into little plastic bags, it was very convincing—even for an ex-addict. Afterward, I threw the props into a bag and brought it home and forgot about it.

Never had the heart to tell her.

V

SISTER MORPHINE

Le Rêve est un seconde vie.
[Dreaming is a second life.]

—*Gérard de Nerval*, "Aurélia,
ou Le Rêve et la vie."

*At this point a question may well have been inad-*vertently raised, if not voiced, and thus may merit address: how did these words end up in front of your eyes? One possible answer is that one morning I woke up in my little hospital bed, not more than a cot, really, in my little hospital room, not more than a cell, really, and I was suddenly bored enough to write these words down in a journal, the words that are now floating before you. I started at the beginning—not the beginning of the volume you currently hold; that beginning was added toward the end. No, I started here, with these words, "at this point," at the beginning, the omphalos and all that, how my mother (as I began writing, in longhand) had graduated from high school in 1910, in Vienna—how long ago that seemed, how far away. And how (I continued) this was such a big deal, for a young woman in Central Europe in 1910; even if it had been a few years later, it would still have been a big deal. So my mom's parents, brimming with pride, wanted to celebrate; they went to the great Hapsburg port of Trieste, and that's how the whole story really began.

They stayed for a week at a hotel with a terrace right on the water. One night my grandfather (he claimed) spent a whole night drinking with James Joyce, who, he said, told him he'd hatched a scheme to import textiles from Ireland that would forever absolve him of financial turmoil. My grandfather covered the tab because, in his words, "From the moment I set eyes upon this man, I knew that while fortune would forever elude him, fame most certainly would not." My grandmother didn't believe it. I like to think it's true. Merely embellished, maybe.

After the week in Trieste, my grandparents put my mom on a steamship to Egypt, for a month-long stay with Uncle Al. The idea was self-improvement as well as celebration: Alexandria, the jewel of the Mediterranean, was the most diverse and cosmopolitan city in the living museum of Egypt. And my mom would perfect her French. And Al was doing well: he'd moved from Austria to Constantinople before the turn of the century to set up emporia. This wasn't that unusual; Austria had long been Central Europe's conduit to the Levant, and there was money to be made there. Al's store became a chain: after Constantinople he opened a second down the Turkish coast, in

İzmir (then Smyrna); a third, moving east, in Aleppo, Syria; a fourth in Alexandria. But my mom's month-long visit became a four-year stay with my father-to-be, an aspiring poet from London. My father's family had been in England for a couple of generations, but they were originally Hungarian Jews, so there was common ground: the binding soil of Central Europe, the binding culture of the Hapsburgs. I'm certain my parents regarded these four years in Alexandria before Ferdinand's death as the loveliest in their lives. How couldn't they? Tennis at the sporting club, gimlets at sunset, the warmth of Alexandrian dusk. My dad had a sinecure at the British Post Office that let him write as much verse as he wanted; my mom, a contralto, sang Maddalena and Cherubino at the Alexandria Opera. Then I was born, and then the world exploded.

My father took us back to London when Britain declared war on the Ottomans, correctly predicting that the British military's deposition of the khedive would ignite a revolution. The irony that he would meet his death two years later during this very conflict needs no underscoring. After my father was killed, my mother and I moved to Budapest, a mid-size apartment on Andrássy Street, four blocks away from the Liszt Academy. Budapest, for her, was a way to extend the marriage in her mind. London would have been impossible; his absence was too obvious. In Budapest, there were distant relatives of my father: perhaps she felt that dim traces of light imply long distances to bright, still-living sources.

She never sang after my father died, but she taught me piano, and by the time I applied for school, I knew I was good enough to get into the Liszt Academy, and I was right. I didn't

Alexandria, Egypt, c. 1920.

think I was good enough to get into Vienna, but I was wrong.
Vienna! Mozart and Beethoven and Mahler and Sibelius.
When I got the letter I ran over to my friend Andy's place (Andy
was my best friend, a dark, slightly melancholic character who
wore bow ties and a mustache and was an excellent violinist,
but we knew he was doomed to a career in law). Vienna! Andy
couldn't believe it. He and the whole gang took me out that
night to this place we loved, a dark restaurant in a basement
where the beautiful Romanian girls would go, and late at night
these terrific folk musicians would play on old instruments,
reed violins and jughorns, hurdy-gurdies and dulcimers. But
we mainly loved it because the owner would let us drink. Drink
we did. Andy ordered a fifth or sixth round and raised his glass
"to Vienna!"

I said, "Vienna? I'm going to Budapest."

A pin dropped. I felt like the whole restaurant was staring at me. I didn't realize it then, but we were what you'd call bourgeois intellectuals, everybody was studying philosophy and history and classics. We were also Hungarian nationalists—except for tonight.

"What's the matter?" I asked.

"What's the matter?" Andy said. "Nothing. I love watching my friends throw their lives away."

"Throwing my life away," I said. "Right. Just like Reiner and Solti and Sándor did, only the most successful musicians in America. I'll study with Bartók, that hack." As the waitress brought our food, deep-fried calves' brains and stuffed cabbage and veal-filled pancakes and cold cherry soup, Andy held my arm. "You're joking, right?" he said. No, I said.

"We're stuck here," Andy said. "You can escape! You're going to die four blocks from where you were born!"

I said, "Andy, I was born in Egypt."

We ate and drank and argued and flirted with the girls and debated the pros and cons of Vienna and Budapest and didn't really talk about some other aspects regarding moving to Vienna in 1934. It isn't that we were avoiding it. We would talk about it, all of us would. Just not that night. But everybody talked about it. But then again you have to understand that people would talk about a lot of things. So often it's only in retrospect that one traces the disease to a symptom, whereas in the heat of the moment every nerve ending of the body is clamoring for one's attention. Perhaps this isn't the worst place to remind ourselves of the astonishingly complex design of one's momentary field of vision, forever bursting (well not forever, but you know what I mean) not only with the immediate stimuli of the present moment—Andy's law-school-ish counterarguments, for example; or the delicious crunch of deep-fried brains; the sharp green eyes of a Romanian girl in a white dress; a newspaper photo, yellow and brittle as a dead moth, of Hitler, taped to the wall; the watery crash of a beater hitting a dulcimer; Andy ordering another round of drinks and laughing and shaking his head. We're bombarded not only with these, but with the recalled stimuli of the past as well. And these two layers wrap around each other like two electric currents encircling some wobbly magnetic pole. Some of these stimuli, both the remembered and the immediate, will, in the future, be remembered, some forgotten; and some of those remembered will, in retrospect, be trivialities: and a few will be History.

•

THE FIRST DAY of classes, I walked by a practice room and heard a violin student playing the opening of Beethoven's Kreutzer Sonata. It was marvelous. The Kreutzer begins with a solo violin; the pianist enters fifteen seconds after, with an A major chord. It was as if I'd never heard an A major chord before, and at that moment I knew I would never be a pianist.

Next, two cold d minor chords, and at that moment I was thrown into despair; what would I be, then?

Next, a whole measure of E dominant seventh, a sign of hope, and I knew I would be a writer.

I peered through the door's small square window and

First page of Beethoven's manuscript of the Kreutzer Sonata for violin and piano, with Beethoven's corrections, 1803.

glimpsed the pianist's face. F major! This, in music, is called a deceptive resolution. The phrase is self-descriptive, really; you're expecting something, and something else happens instead, and it's marvelous. In music, the E chord is "supposed" to lead to an A chord, so when it leads to an F chord instead, colors shift slightly and deepen, like you're suddenly staring through a small square window into the eyes of the girl you know you'll marry. The funny thing is that I was always afraid, even after the wedding, that I wasn't really in love with Valentina, but with that particular F chord, and she just happened to have perfectly coincided with it on the space-time continuum. But I would calm myself by remembering that she, as well as Beethoven, was the creator of that chord—not just her exquisite Bulgarian hands but her very being: not just her exquisite figure but her entire landscape.

·

THIS STORY ISN'T really about my marriage to Valentina, this Bulgarian girl with serious, almost-almond-shaped eyes, low voice, unblemished olive skin, and bony ankles who always seemed to be enveloped in a scent of violets. If it were, I'd relate little anecdotes—like the time we were, the two of us, alone in a practice room at the academy; she was grading papers, and I was fooling around on the piano, stumbling my way through the middle movement of Beethoven's Fourth Piano Concerto. She came over to the piano and sat beside me, eyes twinkling. "Yes," she said, "you can play!" But she took over, as did a kind of dream; she closed her eyes and, referring to the piano, said—

—you see, it *sings*.

But this story isn't about that, so I feel justified in skipping ahead a few years to 1963, when the Rolling Stones signed a record deal for the first time and when I, at the tender age of forty-nine, was for the first time thrown in prison. By then I had a column on music in the most prestigious magazine in Hungary. I'd written a dual profile of two composers I knew, Ligeti and Kurtág. For me, they were the greatest composers in Europe; they divided Europe between them and there was no third.

Ligeti's music was expansive, scored for huge orchestras, and dealt with immense sheets of shimmering sound that seemed to freeze time; Kurtág's music was miniature, employing just a few musicians, neurotically fixated on the tiniest details. Ligeti had fled Hungary for the West after Kádár, the prime minister, crushed the 1956 student uprising; Kurtág stayed. Both Ligeti and Kurtág were Jewish. But Ligeti was sent into a forced labor camp during World War II. His brother had been sent to Mauthausen, and he died. Both of his parents had been sent to Auschwitz. His mother had survived and his father had died. Might these be reasons why Ligeti fled Hungary? I certainly didn't suggest such a thought in my article. So when I received an invitation to the prime minister's office after the article came out, my editor and I had no idea what to expect. I remember waiting with my editor in the plush antechamber of the Office of the Prime Minister, perched on the Danube, about twelve blocks from the apartment Valentina and I had bought on Andrássy Street, two blocks away from the Zeneakadémia, and two blocks away from the apartment in which I grew up. I remember wondering if we were actually going to meet Kádár. We didn't. The minister of culture let us in. We knew him casually. He enjoyed the article, he said. Then he asked if I would be amenable to help the Hungarian government.

Of course, I said. (What does one say?) What can I do?

The charade was quintessential propaganda, Kádár-style. I'd be imprisoned for a week. But my magazine would report—and the national media would repeat—that I was hospitalized for an undisclosed ailment. I'd wear a fake IV; I'd appear, every now and then, on a balcony, in a wheelchair, with a fake catheter sticking out of my chest. After a week, I would miraculously recover, and nothing more would be said of the event. On Friday at midnight, a limo would whisk me home. Did I have any questions? he asked.

Yes, I said. Why not just throw me in prison for a week?

Because the Kádár government, he said, does not imprison writers.

That was the brilliance of Kádár, and in a way—even though I'm certain he killed my friend Andy, people don't just disappear, we all knew Andy participated in the uprising—I do wish I'd met him, just to see how the air reacted when he displaced molecules of it. Of course everyone would decipher the true story. Even if I'd wanted to keep it a secret, it would have been impossible. But Kádár *didn't* want it kept a secret. His power lay precisely in the very transparency of the charade.

I suppose part of me worried. I'm sure I asked myself what would happen if Friday midnight rolled around and there was no limo waiting downstairs; if my "hospitalization" was extended; if the "doctors" had found some type of complication that necessitated another day or two, just to keep me under observation. But when I strolled into the hospital, threw on this hospital gown, when they glued fake IVs to my chest and arms, sat me in a wheelchair and rolled me out to the balcony of my suite—it was very nice, really, like a good hotel—and my editor and I smoked a cigar, I felt this kind of giddy amusement at the sheer absurdity of the situation that I do feel is inimical to Eastern European culture, a temperament that the West will never apprehend.

The one thing I worried about was my mother. She had never fully recovered from the death of my father. I remember once—I think I was around twelve—I awoke in the middle of the night. Someone was crawling past my bedroom door. I lay in bed, frozen, for God knows how long, terrified. Finally I jumped up and swung my door open. My mother, bejeweled and in evening clothes, was dragging herself along the carpeted corridor, humming drawn-out glissandos from the bottom of her register to the peak. "Are you all right?" I asked.

"I'm at the edge," she said. "I think I'm going over the edge. Or at least—I can see the edge."

When she arrived to visit at the hospital I could tell something was wrong—the look of etched concern half-hidden under rudimentary graciousness. She took a seat in a chair of striped canvas that wouldn't have looked out of place on a steamship in 1910. In fact, she herself wouldn't have looked out of place on a steamship in 1910, where, in a sense, she forever was.

We chatted, rather aimlessly, about an article she had been reading about glaciers. Then she glanced at me and asked in a different voice if she could bring me anything, and suddenly she was on the verge of tears.

"You do know this isn't real," I said, but before I'd finished I knew she didn't. How far along she was into senility? Alzheimer's? Something else?

"I'll be back every day," she said, oddly, and she got up and kissed me and left, and I saw her speaking with one of the pretend nurses, and I wondered what exactly the actress employed as the nurse had been instructed to say to those unfortunate souls like my mother who weren't in on the masquerade.

Finally Friday rolled around. By now I had cabin fever. My mother returned. I asked her when she knew she'd marry my father. She didn't answer directly. She spoke of being a couple versus being together, and how that changed things: the subtle recalibrations in the way friends and acquaintances greeted them as they entered social gatherings, the country-house weekends, the piano bars, the shooting parties: a door would open the same way, she said, and then the welcoming gestures would be replicated with a degree of exactitude—the same approach to the handshake, the same curve of the hand through the air, as if algorithmically preordained—that betrayed their artificiality. I realized that a possible definition of love is the sharing of very particular forms of social alienation. Then I wondered if this were the only definition of love. And suddenly this thought made me feel lethargic. Or maybe, out of respect, I wanted to leave my mother alone with these intimate memories and, not physically able to leave the space, opted for sleep, feigned or otherwise. It was eight o'clock at night; I wanted to sleep through the final four hours of my stay, which felt like the last few hours of a very long flight, that mix of anticipation and fatigue.

I opened my eyes to see the long thinner wand gleefully click six degrees to her right, jumping atop her short fatter bedfellow. I congratulated my internal alarm. But no wonder, I thought as I got out of bed; it wasn't as if this time hadn't been inscribed somewhere deep in the folds of whatever part of the brain is responsible for the perception of time's passage. My mom was asleep, in the chair that looked like it belonged on a ship. I nudged her awake as I took off my hospital robe. "We're going," I said.

"Where?" she asked, confused.

"Home. There's a limo outside, waiting."

"No," my mother said, "you're in the hospital."

A pretend nurse walked in, smiled knowingly. I returned her smile, then looked back at my mother and said, "It's okay. My editor's waiting outside in a limo. The hospital story is just a cover—it was the article I wrote. The prime minister wanted to send a message. But we can go now."

My mother shook her head. "No, you're sick. You're in the hospital. On the Upper East Side."

Upper East Side? What was that? "Mom, we're like twelve blocks from Andrássy Street. Valentina's waiting for us."

"Honey," she said, "you can't leave. You're in the hospital. You're very sick."

Suddenly, dread. Everyone had lied to me. My editor, the minister of culture, the prime minister. But of course he had—he'd killed Andy in 1956. I was in prison. My mother was right. I looked around the room. It looked different, suddenly, like a camera lens had been replaced, and the color balance had been adjusted. After years of relative nonchalance, I was experiencing the dark side of Goulash Communism. I realized with horror that since Andy's disappearance I'd been faintly telling myself, "After all, he knew what he was getting into." Meaning the uprising of 1956. But he participated. Why would I pose a threat? My own editor—my employer, my closest intellectual companion, the father-figure that eased me into society—betrayed me? Of course. He sold me out, just as he had surely sold out others. How else had he uniquely been able to procure intellectual freedom for the magazine? By forsaking his son.

Ligeti got out, I thought. I glanced out the door. Another pretend nurse walked into the room. She left the door open. She stood there, listening, saying nothing. I couldn't see guards in the yellow hallway behind her. At first that was a relief—but then I realized that was worse. Where are they hiding? I silently calculated the time it would take to run on foot from Gellért Hill to Andrássy Street. It was midnight, so the streets would be empty. It was dark. I had to get to Valentina, get her out of here, head to—where?

I felt the first hints of panic. "We've got to get out of here, Mom," I said, ripping the eight fake IVs out of my chest. Fake blood went everywhere. They really thought of everything, I remember thinking. "This is turning into a very dangerous situation."

But it was too late. The pretend nurses grabbed me, forced me back into the bed. My mother, powerless. I thought about Valentina, our marriage in Bulgaria, the Kreutzer Sonata. I thought about Andy laughing when I said I wasn't going to Vienna, and how we had a slightly similar night years later when he told me—in the same restaurant!—that he was working for the Resistance. And how his disappearances became first more frequent, then longer, and then he was gone. How superior, public executions. At least you know. His wife probably still hopes. Where was Valentina? I hadn't heard from her in a while, I realized. Meanwhile, my mother was talking. She was holding me, going on and on, a calm, hysteric rant. How long had it been since I'd seen Valentina? I was sitting down on the bed. The fake blood was streaming down my chest. Too watery, I thought. Looks like red water. These special effects teams in 1963. How much are they being paid? Goddamn unions. (I sound like my father.) Nobody's going to believe this, I said to myself, rubbing my hand against my slippery chest in fury. See, it's slippery. It should be sticky. Effects will be so much better, won't they. And then digital. In the 1990s. More pretend nurses now, holding me down. When was it—the last time I saw Valentina? Why can't I remember? The pretend nurses are sticking needles back into my fake wounds, there are cables attached to the needles. The wonderful thing about Valentina is how beautifully she aged. That was a relief. You never know, when you marry a girl. When you date someone, you're dating her present self, but when you marry someone, you're marrying someone known only to your future self. It's the bone structure. The Bulgarian mixture of Slavic and Russian and Greek and Macedonian and Tartar and Hun and Turk and God knows what else. The olive skin, the almond serious eyes. She could pass for Persian. She is a religious woman. I'm not. She goes to church. A believer, yes. She believes. The book of Job and all that. Question it poses is, why does it exist? Funny. It exists to pose the question of why it exists. Because it shouldn't exist, a book like that. By all rights, it shouldn't exist. So why *does* it exist? In order to ask that question.

They're pretending to inject me with something. I almost want to act as if I feel the needle going in. Play along. Needles are hollow things with mouths. My mother won't stop talking, she's over the edge now, like she said that night when she was crawling outside my bedroom in a black cocktail dress, wearing diamonds that gleamed in the blue darkness; soon she'll be getting the time wrong, she'll think it's morning when the sun's going down, I can see us in the future at a diner in America, me sitting across the little table from her aged wounded face, her blank eyes staring into the dull spoon she pretends to float like a ship on the surface of the coffee, a tiny wine-dark sea all her own, nestled in the bay enclosure of a paper cup ringed with a blue and white geometric band filled with meanders for fear of a void. More pretend nurses are running in. In their white gowns, they look ridiculous. They look like high school drama students somewhere in the American Midwest attempting Greek tragedy; they have the effortless, self-conscious beauty of awkward youth, rushing too quickly into a Greek vase pose, their anxious eyes searching for their parents in the overheated auditorium. It's getting confusing. But I can use that to my advantage, as soon as I take a little rest; no, I'll pretend to take a nap, the actors will relax, everyone will fall asleep, and I'll just walk right out as if nothing happened. The only way to deal with these types of threats is to be utterly relaxed. Not even to seem relaxed, but to be relaxed. Just seeming isn't enough. You can never petition the Lord by prayer. My father thought there were three good examples of English: Shakespeare and Eliot and the

King James. But where is Valentina? My wife. I always wondered to whom those two words would refer. Valentina. She has faith. We never discuss it. We had a religious wedding, an Eastern Orthodox wedding. Is it Greek Orthodox or Russian Orthodox? Bulgarian is written in Cyrillic. So exotic. When we met and would make love she'd murmur in Russian. I felt like James Bond. I love the way her inner thigh bone joins her groin. She knows I don't believe. She never brings it up, never tries to change me, to convert me. We'll walk into a church somewhere and we'll see the same icons but they appear differently to us. The fake blood coming out of the wounds, the painted blood on the painted sculptures, she sees all that differently. I know it's fake when I see it. She thinks it's real blood. She sees it as real. But I know it's fake blood. But the thing is what's New York? Because my mother's saying as if it's important "you're in the hospital, you're in New York, you're being treated for

·

IT WAS SOMETHING about those two words—"New York"—that jolted me out of the morphine delusion. "New York" existed somewhere in a distant corner of my mind, but how did that jive with my studies at the Liszt Academy, my job, my editor, Valentina above all? And all of that crystalline detail?

When it came back, it came back block by block. Literally. I mean the first thing that came into my head was the intersection of Sixty-Eighth Street and York. So first was geographic

Budapest and the Danube.

location: the Upper East Side of Manhattan. Wouldn't you think it'd be something else? Recognizing my mother, for instance? Or remembering my name? The self? No, it was where the self was positioned on the surface of the earth. I saw the subway map in my head, and I zoomed out, saw an overhead satellite image of the island, then the country. Then, for some reason, I thought of Columbia University. Bartók taught at Columbia. I was finishing a music degree at Columbia when I got the diagnosis, and I was teaching a class there. That was the reason I was in New York. Not really, but at this point, that would do. Then the year, I think.

Then after that everything hit at once. It was a soft blow. I wasn't happy to be in the hospital having a bone marrow transplant, vomiting thick green bile, being unable to swallow my own saliva, unable to move my mouth without cracking the calcified, thick-and-white-and-hard-as-porcelain mucus lining that coated my gastrointestinal tract, claustrophobic, perhaps dying, fearing insanity. But on the other hand, I liked my life; I liked my childhood, my parents, my brother, my city, my decade, my era; I liked the fact that I'd lived in France, my friends, the girls I'd dated; I liked growing up in Milwaukee, with its South Side that looked like Warsaw and its North Side that looked like Mulberry Street; I liked my friends in high school, my first girlfriend, that cute Armenian girl and the time we went out for Italian food and saw a double feature of *The 39 Steps* and *The Third Man*; I liked the fact that I was in my thirties, I thought that was a pretty cool time of life; I really liked how my father had taught me about writing, how he had shared these great books with me; I liked the United States, how it was a strange country in so many ways, but really had produced a lot of things we can be proud of; I liked the fact that Louis Armstrong (of whom that junkie deadbeat Billie Holliday, who can boast coauthorship of at most a handful of songs, unconscionably said, "Of course he Toms, but he Toms from the heart"; who gave away more than half his lifetime income in spite of the fact that he was born penniless, out of wedlock, to a son and a daughter of slaves; who as a child hauled coal in Back of Town, a squalid slum which he later called "the heart of good old New Orleans, something to live for"; who was one of MLK's crucial financial patrons, and anonymously, out of modesty; who turned down State Department funding to protest what he perceived as Eisenhower's inaction in the face of the desegregation movement; who was the musician that, at age sixty-three, dislodged the Beatles' unique fourteen-week, three-song reign at numbers one, two, and three on the charts; who bought his first trumpet with a loan from a Russian Jew junkyard owner in whose honor he wore a Star of David pendant every day for the rest of his life) was American; I liked the fact that we had computers now, that the Beatles and the Rolling Stones and Led Zeppelin had already come out; I liked digital recording techniques, and iTunes; I liked single malt Scotch, and rainy weather and fireplaces, and the fact that my father had taught me chess; I liked how I had put all the Mozart operas on my computer at home in iTunes, and had organized them by year—it was cool to see them arranged like that, to see how incredible it was that he wrote all that music in such a short span of time, really. Oh and that's right—music! I really thought it was actually pretty cool that I had learned how to write music, how I had written these pieces—I did a quick inventory of them in my mind, ran through some of them in fast-forward.

But what about Valentina?

They took me off the morphine that night, switched me to fentanyl.

•

ANOTHER FUNNY THING: not only my wholesale belief in the delusion, but the fact that I actually thought I'd been writing the whole thing down. In reality, here's what I wrote, between May 18 and June 3, when I was on the morphine drip:

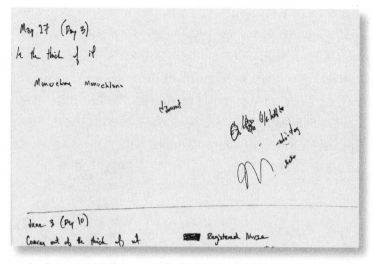

And my entire memoir, the history of my parents, my marriage, my imprisonment—let's get a closer look at that:

Just two entries, scribbles. I wonder whether during the delusion I experienced the narrative the way I remember it, like a story; or whether the entire thing, present and past, wife and parents and grandparents, was created in a single, synchronous flash that overwhelmed my mind the instant before I tore the IVs out of my chest, and the nurses sounded the alarm.

Compare these pages to a page from my pre-delusional self's journal, just a few days before, with a fairly accurate sketch from memory of the Bastille in Paris, where I'd lived, and where (I'd just been notified) there was some chance of having a new work of music produced, a sort of avant-garde opera (it ended up not working out, which is too bad, because apparently they were talking to David Lynch about doing sound design).

And a map I drew of my neighborhood:

Or Exhibit B, a diagram of the electromagnetic spectrum, in a minimalist style. Light is part of the electromagnetic spectrum.

Most radiation treatment in the context of oncology uses X-rays, which fall near the top of the piano keyboard of the electromagnetic spectrum: Uranus between the Saturn of ultraviolet and the Neptune of gamma rays. (Remember that— as I note in extremely disciplined hand, since I'm talking about science here, not art—the electromagnetic spectrum is thus called because its waves have both electric and magnetic components; and the physics controlling these waves is electrodynamics. This represents my sum total knowledge of this subject, so we shall move on.)

Electromagnetic radiation

gamma rays

x-rays

ultraviolet

"light" from blue
↓
red

infrared

microwave

radio waves FM
↓
or
AM

long radio waves

81 octaves

"electromagnetic"; since the waves have both electric and magnetic components. the physics controlling these waves is electrodynamics.

Now were we to approach the delusion as a dream, and if we were to some extent Freudians (which we are, of course, we eminent Victorians), many elements are clearly recognizable as "residue," as Freud called the distorted figurations of objects we fear or desire that our waking selves refuse to acknowledge, leaving that task to the unconscious, including Dorothy Gale's unconscious in *The Wizard of Oz.* In this film (premiered, incidentally, in Wisconsin, in 1939), a twelve-year-old girl, traumatized by the realization that she is homosexual, experiences an elaborate delusion in which her dreary, homophobic relatives and friends in Depression-era Kansas are transformed into celebratory marchers in a sort of gay pride parade in Technicolor. (Now I'm mixing Jung in with Freud, but who cares. "I'm a writer, not a psychologist," he growled from downstairs; and she, just like the time before, and surely just like the next, sighed and pretended not to hear him. Wait, hold on, I'm not writing fiction.)

In real life, my mother is a gifted musician, just as she was in the morphine dream; and she suffered an emotional breakdown not unlike that experienced by my Viennese mother. The thing about my European family living in pre–World War I Alexandria was unconsciously cribbed from Eric Hobsbawm's *The Age of Empire*, a book I'd been reading in the hospital. My father hadn't been killed, but he had died. Budapest? A city I love, where I've eaten deep-fried calves' brains for dinner, and heard folk musicians playing hammer dulcimers. I'd had a good friend in high school named Andy, who was a gifted musician but went on to study law. The Liszt Academy stands in for Northwestern University's School of Music—a separate school, rather than a department, thus nearly a conservatory, rare for universities. Valentina was based on a college girlfriend who really is Bulgarian, really is a wonderful pianist, really is exceedingly lovely. The composers are real, I've met both of them; their stories are real; I've really written music journalism. Et cetera.

In other words, the morphine acted as the classic unreliable narrator, unleashing this elaborate yarn in the great tradition of Vladimir Nabokov, William Faulkner, and David Fincher. But if the elements of the story—the characters and motifs, the place settings and odd little details—are distortions of things I fear and desire in real life, then, as my father would have said, what's this movie *about*?

It's about guilt. I'd transferred the notion of hospitalization for treatment of an illness to imprisonment for having written an article about music. My own ambivalence about life choices—that is, the pursuit of a career in the arts and humanities, rather than in finance—thus surfaces in a classic twist ending, in a most unexpected, colorful, and terrifying manner.

The guilt of the ill—especially the guilt of those who have done nothing to help create their state—is a theme on which we've touched, and on which we're sure to touch again, but for now consider the interesting notion that if a person finds himself or herself in a situation for no reason, he or she will go to quite extraordinary lengths to create a reason. If there is no agency, we will create an agency—even (especially!) a malignant one. My illness had nothing to do with lifestyle; it was a roll of the dice, as the poet Mallarmé would have put it; it was a numbers thing, a genetic mutation somewhere that surfaces so rarely that natural selection grudgingly opens the velvet rope. I am not responsible for my illness, nor was I ever responsible; rape victims are not responsible for being raped; civilians who are captured and tortured by despots as a show of power are not responsible for being captured and tortured: we should have learned this by now. This is why God told Saint Beckett to walk the lands of the earth, preaching the Christian doctrine of Absurdity: to absolve His children of our sins, of our guilt. But we wouldn't listen, so God was forced to do more. God found a Parisian pimp named Prudent and asked him to murder Saint Beckett, for no reason. At first, Prudent refused: he had no prior relationship with the saint, and had absolutely no motive for doing him harm. But it was, after all, God's order. So Prudent sought down Saint Beckett and stabbed him in the chest. The reason God did not let Saint Beckett die was so that Saint Beckett could confront his attacker and ask him, why? And God had Prudent reply,

Je ne sais pas, Monsieur. Je m'excuse.

In English:

Dunno. Sorry.

•

THERE ARE SEVERAL consequences for all this.

We've covered Freud and Darwin. So that just leaves Nietzsche. The crystalline clarity of this morphine delusion proves, perhaps, the Nietzschean maxim that "some situations are so bad that to remain sane is insane." I had always enjoyed, even as a very young child, a rich dream-life. Many of my experiences in dreams, in fact, have been far more vivid than some real-life experiences; not only do dreams account for some of the most emotionally engaged moments of my life, but—and this is somewhat embarrassing to reveal, but I'm being perfectly honest—they account for *every* moment in my life in which I've felt politically engaged. It's a feeling I've never been able to recapture in waking life, to my great disappointment. (Then again, if I spent 1 percent of my time actually reading about politics, informing myself as a responsible citizen, instead of writing all the time about nothing, and reading books about Ezra Pound, whom nobody even knows anymore, let alone cares about, I might be able to fulfill this part of my life.) And primarily it's for this reason that I'm typically tempted to consider dreams as unmediated, sacrificing intellectual gradations for intensity. But so many moments in waking life are unmediated as well—love, states of intoxication, listening to great music, et cetera—and I've had, on the other hand, analytical dreams, dreams that continue the day's work, problem-solving dreams (these, to my mind, are failed dreams). So what, exactly, separates a sharp memory of early childhood, say, from a morphine delusion, or an image seen in a dream from an image read in a book? They're all equally tangible, equally intangible products of electrochemical signaling. About twenty minutes ago, for example, I awoke suddenly, for no apparent reason. It's about four thirty in the morning. I often awake like this now; I have ever since the transplant. I opened my eyes and the blue-grey light of early dawn, dim but secure, was distinct as porcelain. Then I realized it wasn't daybreak at all, but fluorescent light emanating from one of the tallwindowed artists' studios (wait, there are still artists in

New York?) facing my apartment, across the narrow canyon of lower Broadway. (In the original draft of *The Waste Land*, Eliot writes of sailors seeing by starboard "something which we knew must be a dawn— / a different darkness," and his friend Mr. Pound excised the line.)[7] That was the first realization, the thing about the light. The second: for the first few moments of wakefulness, I had entirely forgotten my hospital experience, the very subject of this book; and I'd only realized I'd forgotten it at the sudden appearance in my mind's eye of the image—as vengeful as an illusion—of my hospital room's wall, and at first I interpreted the image as a dreamt one. But the hospital wall was and is no dream, it was and is memory, and for the subsequent few moments this fact was dumbfounding; as the false dream gradually took proper form as true memory, it seemed to be a memory impossibly distant, a memory, perhaps, belonging to someone else. It couldn't be my memory. Not yet. Pound once wrote a poem called "Envoi," which begins by addressing a "dumb-born book," and goes on to have a female voice quote or echo or rewrite or pay homage to or rip off another poem by the seventeenth-century English poet Edmund Waller. And Hugh Kenner, that wonderful aforementioned critic who people don't read enough of these days (people couldn't possibly read him enough, but alas, they live their lives as responsible citizens, reading about politics), describes the poem as "in a time so far declined from Waller's that the lady singing Waller's song does not know his name."[8] Pound is not the lady, and the lady doesn't know Edmund Waller; but she sings his song.

I think the fact that I had entirely forgotten, for a few moments, my hospitalization is a good sign, and the fact that I misinterpreted the recollection of the hospital room's wall as a dream is another good sign. Isn't that mental health? Ultimately a healthy person *correctly* assigns electrochemical signalings to dream or to imagination, to memory or to delusion. But before the healthy person does this, doesn't the healthy person also temporarily *miscategorize*—especially if such miscategorization might serve as a self-saving mechanism? What else, after all, is creativity, if not self-permission to get something wrong, in order to subsequently reorder that something to get it right, like the little boy Freud saw, hiding his toys so that he could lose them, so he could have something to seek? With that thought: back to sleep. It's twenty to five. I can regrasp sleep; it's tangible, within my reach. No problem. And now I remember I'd been dreaming, not of the hospital but of something else, I remember what it was and I kid you not: it was and is the end of this chapter. I'd been dreaming about reading exactly what I'm writing right now. I hadn't written it; I was reading it, and what I'm doing at this moment is transcribing it—trying to be as accurate a court reporter as Mohammed's scribe. (I'd read that phrase, in the dream. I kid you not. This parenthetical was not in the dream. Okay, back to the dream.) The dream was about voice: this is a memoir, and to tell a memoir, especially a memoir of the experiences I have to describe, I have to adopt a voice other than my own, and speak through it. (As I mistook my memory of the hospital wall for someone else's memory; as Pound is not the lady singing the song that is not hers, not that she knows. This parenthetical, incidentally, wasn't in the book in the dream, either. And the artist has turned off his fluorescent light, but now there is, in fact, the blue-grey light of early dawn, dim but secure, distinct as porcelain. From blackness to blue-grey dreaming to red noontime life, back to blue-grey sunset back to blackness. There will be repetition in this account. But back to transcribing the chapter in the dream. Here's how it ended. I kid you not:) It's my voice and not my voice. So what's true, what's false? What if I grabbed a light-blue highlighter and highlighted the true statements, left the false statements alone? I would highlight this one, then. This one I wouldn't touch. This one is true. This one—not. If I were to be perfectly honest. I kid you not.

VI

WAS PICASSO SMART?

Golaud: *Je dis une chose très simple. Je n'ai pas d'arrière-pensée; Si j'avais une arrière-pensée, pourquoi ne la dirais-je pas?*

I'm saying something very simple. There's no subtext. If I had a subtext why wouldn't I just say it?

—*Maurice Maeterlinck, the libretto for Debussy's opera* Pelléas et Mélisande

How I'd wanted to go step by step through the story, chapter by chapter, block by block, regimented, writing a draft and polishing a block until lo and woe and behold there it stands: the simple story in the sunlight, a line of polished blocks. So much for that.

You've probably forgotten, for example, that when I was talking about *Don Giovanni* and the Rolling Stones' *Some Girls* I also brought up Paul Klee—how he was enamored of the Mozart opera, how he once inscribed a painting with a list of his sexual conquests. One of my major "security blankets" during the hospitalization was an old art book on Klee that I'd inherited from my parents. Why was it such a comfort?

First of all, obviously, because I, along with so many others, admire his art. It's pleasurable to look at, and finding sources of pleasure is an important aspect of dealing with high levels of pain.

But along with my love for his art is my love for what I imagine he was *as a person*. Isn't that odd? I don't just like his art, I like *him*, as an imaginary friend. When I realized this, I found this was very odd, for I normally see myself as an early twenty-first-century, darkly brooding, edgy, raw post-postmodernist, not a seventeenth-century, teleologically minded, moral sentimentalist like the Third Earl of Shaftesbury, or Holden Caulfield. But then I realized that my favorite artists are those I imagine would be nice people to know. And that's fucked up. David Foster Wallace wrote that "watching his scenes I again felt that I admired [David] Lynch as an artist and from a distance but would have no wish to hang out in his trailer or be his friend."9 On the other hand, when I met Lynch I found him to be extremely nice; I got a really good feeling from him. Unlike DFW, I *would* like to be his friend. Some of Lynch's subject matter is pretty disturbing, but some of the things I've been writing about are pretty disturbing too. And I wouldn't like it if someone read my book and said, I admire him as a writer, but I would have no wish to meet someone who wrote things like that, or to be friends with someone who would write things like that. When I was writing this, I gave a draft of part of this book to a friend in publishing, and she said she thought the writing was good but warned me that if it's published "you won't be able to have regular relationships anymore." What the hell did she mean by that? Maybe the stuff about girls? And then—as a matter of fact—she never talked to me again. And

I wondered, maybe I shouldn't publish it? This issue of the inter-connectedness of guilt and fear and writing was, as I tried to demonstrate, the heart of my morphine delusion, and it was—as we'll see—a major preoccupation of my father when he quit his job and devoted himself to writing, and was afraid he was upsetting everyone. He wasn't upsetting me. I told him that.

(And for that matter, David Foster Wallace wrote some pretty disturbing things as well, and it's the same thing—I admire his writing *and* I would have liked to have been his friend, and when he killed himself I was extraordinarily upset and felt as if I had lost a good friend; and I wish he were still around so that I could ask him about this. I know he'd reply.)

(And needless to say the most obvious example of good art-ist slash bad person is Pound. How could you want to meet someone who said over the radio, on April 30, 1942,

> Don't start a pogrom. That is, not an old-style killing
> of small Jews. That system is no good, whatever. Of
> course, if some man had a stroke of genius, and could
> start a pogrom up at the top. I repeat . . . if some man
> had a stroke of genius, and could start a pogrom up at
> the top.[10]

And yet we read that years later Allen

> Ginsberg had taken the master's hand and leaning
> over had kissed him, gracefully and naturally, on the
> right cheek. Pound appeared greatly moved. As he
> turned to walk into the house, he gazed a last time

into the younger poet's eyes and said, "I should have been able to do better." Then he stepped across the threshold and was gone from sight.")

Anyway, the third reason the Klee book was such a comfort stems from my strong association of this particular copy of this particular book with my childhood and my parents, whose collection of art books was a source of fascination for my preliterate self. In all probability my parents hadn't intentionally hidden the books, but as I moved, as a child, from the periwinkle foyer, where guests from the outside were greeted and from the inside were bid farewell, through the vaguely Iberian, stucco arched entryway, finally reaching the living room, all blacks and deep reds—this was where the expensive furniture was; this was where adults would sit after dinner, lowball glasses held over crossed legs; this was where I, as a baby, had been forbidden to tread, a prohibition that had never officially been lifted—I nonetheless had the distinct sense that I was traversing some precarious threshold. The voluptuousness and the silence were tangible there: the odd sensation of being simultaneously cloaked and unveiled: the art books weren't on open shelves, but tucked inside a cylindrical occasional table of solid walnut that doubled as an end table for a Venetian blown-glass lamp. It opened not with hinged cabinet doors but with curved retractable shutters, rather like a tambour desk: sliding the pleated panels open released the delicious odors of wood, furniture polish, and the pungent aroma of old books: sweet almond-vanilla tempered with the slight touch of mildew. And what books! I hadn't yet learned to read. I remember what English looked like then: paragraphs were solid blocks of grey, but when I looked closer they would fall apart, delicately, into spindly tessellations. (And like I said before, I have no memory of not knowing how to read music. Music held.) If the words were indecipherable, the potency of the glossy, hand-fastened plates of Klees and Picassos and de Koonings more than compensated. They represented nothing less than the veiled mystery of my parents' life together before I had existed; they represented, in fact, my parents' complicity in my very coming to existence. (In other words, those books, and for that matter my parents' record collection, equally cryptic, represented the mystery of sex, which is to the virgin what, later, death will be to the spoilt.) I've already talked about this, but what I haven't said is the fact that, reading the Klee book during my fifth or maybe sixth chemo, I hit upon a passage I'd long forgot I'd read. It states that Klee, late in life, was haunted by the question of whether he had given eroticism the proper weight in his work as a whole. What a question! Particularly coming from an abstract, plastic artist—an artist who doesn't deal in words. Because those who don't deal in words, at first glance, seem to me to not have to think about the question of sex as those who think in words do, precisely because sex is not a question until it's put into words. While Roth and Bellow and Updike and Erica Jong and Norman Mailer *think* about sex, Picasso *has* sex. Which brings up the question of whether Picasso was *smart*.

"Was Picasso *smart*?" a brilliant young woman asked me once, long ago. I knew exactly what she meant. (O what gorgeous young minds we had, smooth as sanded sandalwood. One afternoon, we'd driven across a black bridge, over water.)

After all, painters like Picasso and Klee can get away with the casual epigram, the tossed-off aphorism, but writers, uniquely and unjustly burdened by the weight of words, will inevitably be snared. Try paging through Bartlett's. You'll find the painters' quotes are startlingly brilliant, effortless, unlike favorite quotations by Eliot and Nietzsche and Kafka and the great Romanian aphorist Cioran, which seem to have been unearthed laboriously. "Art is the elimination of the unnecessary" (Picasso). "Imitate nothing" (Klee). "Some painters transform the sun into a yellow spot, others transform a yellow spot into the sun" (Picasso). "Color and I are one" (Klee). "Everything you can imagine is real" (Picasso). Aha. Yes, a painter, a plastic artist, a musician would say something like that, wouldn't he. And consider the counter-proposal of the man of letters: Alexander Theroux's devastating final sentence on the 878th page of his latest novel, *Laura Warholic*: "Dreams, by definition, do not come true."

The book on Klee was published the old-fashioned way. Like the *New York Times* tirelessly points out every week or so in an article about one or another of the arts, it's not that nobody has the money to hand-insert plates anymore, it's just that there's no longer a market for it. (I don't need my local paper to remind me over and over that pursuing a career in the arts is risky. That's what parents are for, in high school. And by the way, *New York Times*, there's no longer a market for you either.) The text is written by a German art historian named Will Grohmann, and it's so refreshingly free of the contemporary art critic's second thoughts, irony, and deconstructive analysis. Like how Grohmann writes that Klee's range of reading is "awe-inspiring"; the young painter's "maturity of judgment is astonishing"; Klee "speaks of the most abstract matters in vividly graphic language"; indeed, "only a man with so rich a store of images and anticipations was capable of producing works so entirely new." Grohmann tells us that in 1906, in Munich, at the age of twenty-seven, Klee married a pianist named Lily Stumpf. (Fortunately, Grohmann refers to her as Lily, not Stumpf.) Around this time, Klee was making etchings, and his former professor, a guy named Struck (Struck? Stumpf?), liked them enough to facilitate their exhibition. One of them is called *Virgin in a Tree*. Klee wrote Lily that this work "may suggest something true enough: that enforced virginity, so highly praised, is good for nothing."

Sixteen years later, Klee created a pen and watercolor work entitled *Analysis of Various Perversities*. Mr. Grohmann's demureness strikes the present-day reader as charming, and ultimately as bewildering, as his choice of comma over semicolon after the first clause of his opening sentence, betraying his discomfort.

> Nothing was alien to Klee, he was even interested, though not overly so, in sexual problems. To the extent that he saw them from outside, he did not think the love life of human beings very different from that of other living beings; to the extent that he was involved personally, he often felt that he was neutral. He wondered whether, in the end, people would believe he had taken too little account of such matters. His attitude to the erotic was something else; no one will

Paul Klee, *Analysis of Various Perversities*, 1922.

maintain, surely, that he lacked Eros, but Klee himself often doubted that he had given it its proper place
in his work as a whole.

That's the sentence I was talking about before. What's coinci-
dental is that the watercolor in question pictures a doctor at
work. "The medical and experimental are brought to the fore,"
Mr. Grohmann writes, "presenting us with a kind of laboratory
with much apparatus."[12] I suppose my hospital room was a kind
of laboratory; there was certainly much apparatus, things stuck
in my chest, my arms, the catheter implanted in the chest leading straight to an artery. Baudelaire wrote that "the act of love
strongly resembles torture or surgery." My young, brilliant pain
management MD—but here, unprepared, we are presented with
the intentionally unemphatic entrance of the real Not Her Real
Name. Obviously Caroline was not Caroline's real name, but
neither was Caroline not the real Not Her Real Name; just as
Sophie (not her real name) was not the real Not Her Real Name.
The true Not Her Real Name—I've saved the four-word, tetra-
grammatonical epithet in all its capitalized glory for the one
who deserves it: epithets are, by one definition, contemptuous:
let the penalty match the transgression. Not Her Real Name: or
Nothereal, as I'm going to call her for short, for convenience. I
deserve a little ease at this point. (Alexander Theroux even said
once, probably more than once, that revenge was the "single
most informing element of great world literature," not "love and
war, with which themes . . . it has more than passing acquaintance.")[13] Nothereal: a word that looks—although I've never pro-

nounced it, only written it down—like it would rhyme, ironically, with "ethereal," since she was anything and everything but ethereal, real, all too real: the real Nothereal, a word whose secondary characteristics include a resemblance to "gonorrhea" and "guttural" and "Notting Hill"; these secondary characteristics are less ironic, although the person to which the word points was, and I assume remains, physically disease free, elegantly articulate, and, much to her eternal dismay, was neither raised on Clarendon Cross nor, for that matter, able to physically contribute to the assault of persons with darker pigmentation (to the best of my knowledge, anyway).*

When exactly did she walk into the hospital room that first time? It must have been after Sophie. It was before the morphine delusion, obviously, because, as I mentioned, she was on the pain management team. So it was before I even started the morphine. It must have been fairly early on, then, when I was still cogent, appeared normal. I kept my hair for quite a while, through the first few high-dose chemotherapy rounds. I'm rewinding a bit, to that first glimpse.

It's funny, with Nothereal the whole thing quite literally started with the part and worked outward to the whole, rather than the reverse, and looking back, this in itself may have been the first of the red flags to come, like pylons (also called "witches'

---

* Notting Hill, a fashionable section of London, was also the scene of some particularly nasty race riots in the late 1950s, which began when a bunch of white, working-class hooligans attacked a young, white Swedish woman whose boyfriend was Jamaican. The woman, whose name was Majbritt Morrison, wrote a memoir on the incident called *Jungle West 11*.

hats") on the highway: at first a single spot of safety orange shocks against the horizonless façade of grey-white concrete and concrete-colored sky. Then two, then three. Their frequency increases on the upswing of a parabolic curve—a section of a cone, come to think of it—even as the velocity of your vehicle decreases, until the point of minimum vehicular speed coincides with the point of maximum traffic cone frequency and you slowly roll past the peak of the curve with the ambulance and the stretchers, and you try to try and fail to try to avert your eyes.

(After all the flags and cones and the final catastrophe, a month after that, she sent me a postcard, from Greece. "I had to escape to my favorite place," she wrote, in her curiously square penmanship. She used a blue ballpoint pen. That was where the instant recognition, the immediate empathy, the sense of warmth and the fantasy of some shared past all led. There's never any doubt about that recognition, the feeling of relief is so strong, in accordance with how dearly it's desired. "It is painful," she wrote, "but I think I can handle pain." It's a mirror, essentially. Just like the Greeks said.)

She walked into the room for the first time, and the part of Nothereal's whole in question was, to the best of my recollection, a vermillion, classic patent leather peep-toe pump outfitted with a heel of (I'll wager) three inches. Thus it was less a question of form (as if!) than color. Scarlet is unofficially prohibited by the "color psychologists" that hospitals and prisons hire, at God only knows what rates, to employ Pepto-Bismol pink and Slim-Fast ecru, as tasteless as the food is colorless, to calm patients and prisoners, soothe their eyes and souls during that interval of time before they find themselves on the way out, whichever the way out is. Nothereal's ruby slippers ordained their owner, then, as an iconoclast, a purveyor of audacity: this is the color of blood, ambition, Che Guevara, the Roman Catholic Church, and the stop sign. And one might say that the brilliant point of the self-covered heel glimpsed under the hem of the starched white hospital robe was, in a sense, the first hint of the piercing cry of pleasure and, later, outrage that was to come. I really did look up from the shoes to the face, inadvertently inverting the direction of the origins of fetishism, so I was both mocking it and acknowledging it. Sometimes a pocket is just a pocket, but sometimes the whole is contained in the part, as sometimes the entire weight of the female body, say, is concentrated on two single points: fashion inflicts a fine violence against the woman's body, as any true member of the *haute couture* culture knows and, for that matter, freely admits. Surely Carine Roitfeld, the celebrated former editor of *Paris Vogue*, knows the name of Vanessa Duriès. So if this initial encounter were a painting, it would not be a Klee, not even a Picasso; we would have to look to the perversity of the Surrealists who, like Picasso, took women apart, but unlike him never put them back together. I couldn't help it, though. The shoes and the face were all I had to go on so far, because the rest was whited out. It added up to Italian: dark eyelids, quick dash of hair, the high cheekbones and olive skin. I complimented her on her shoes. This type of thing, incidentally, really does work—it's just like in the movies and on TV, the stretcher pauses to let the patient crack a joke to the kindly surgeon, and an angelic black nurse smiles and the skin around her eyes crinkles in close-up; this cadence is then cut short by the percussive jolt of the single-action hermetically sealed swing doors, and there's no turning back from the operating room. It's the patient who must reassure his caretakers, not the reverse. Take the case of Willem de Kooning, our gentlest poet of sexual horror, and the last great painter only in that narrow sense of "great painters," on his deathbed in East Hampton. He couldn't use the stairs; his diet was through an IV; one of his ex-wives, although he didn't know it, was dead, and another he couldn't recognize.

> Since his condition had deteriorated dramatically, no one was allowed to visit him anymore. The last of his old friends stopped seeing him around 1989. Molly Barnes [an ex-lover] noted that he no longer raised his head to look at her. But she was amazed to hear him mutter, "Nice legs."[14]

When I complimented Nothereal on her shoes, she, fashion-conscious, was flattered. I asked her if she was Italian.

She said, Close.

I said, Let me guess, Greek?

No, but I'm in love with Greece.

Hungarian?

Not too bad. Serbian.

Oh and that made sense: the serious, almost-almond-shaped eyes, slightly Oriental, a touch of the Turk: unblemished olive skin, as if I'd met her before. I'm in love with Serbia, I said. (True!) "Really?" she asked. How odd that we were on our way; everyone in the room, a couple of nurses, noticed it too, I could tell: I'd looked at them for verification.

That night I had a dream about her. We were standing together under an immense dome, which itself was encircled by four smaller domes. We were gazing at a fresco that depicted the Resurrection. Christ was painted emerging through a gleaming archway that framed him perfectly. Two supplicants were kneeling on either side of Him, each softly taking a hand. The one on the left was wearing a white robe; the one on the right, red. Above Christ's head, two words were inscribed. The words were spelled with an alphabet that seemed to flicker between Latin and Cyrillic. The strange beauty of the fresco—not Italian, not Greek, not Turkish—struck me as unsurpassed and profoundly moving. Odd, because I'm not religious. Then we walked outside, into midwinter. We stood alongside this silvery building of five domes, a towering dome set upon four domes, situated on a hill overlooking a city of small buildings that formed a kind of tessellation. In the distance was an incongruously modern sports arena. All was snow, ice, and blinding sunlight, an Antarctic brilliance that was almost painful, as brilliant as light hitting a splintery shard of anthracite: we were holding hands.

The next morning I mentioned the dream to her. Have you been to Belgrade? she murmured.

I had indeed. We had been in the Temple of Saint Sava, in Belgrade, the largest Eastern Orthodox church not just in Serbia or in Eastern Europe but in the entire world, and neither of

The Temple of Saint Sava (detail), Belgrade.

us needed to consult the psychoanalyst on staff to figure out what the dream meant.

I know it sounds like the nurse and the wounded soldier; or two doubles of Narcissus, vainly staring at a pool of black, undisturbed water; or the twin masks of delusion and pathology. But actually it wasn't any of those things. Had it been, there'd be no need to write about it. It was simple; we knew each other, were glad to have finally met, and wanted to be around each other. We wanted to have conversations. But now there might not be enough time: this time we weren't too young. We both knew this; our eyes would narrow about it, in a good way. As a result, we wrapped around each other as swiftly as two electric currents encircling some wobbly magnetic pole.

I recall that her visits after that became at first lengthier, only later more frequent. Each appearance was more quietly joyous than the last. Do I imagine that she was already making the occasional reference to Jews? Surely not just my imagination and I just as surely took them as completely innocuous. But if I took them as innocuous, why would I imagine I remember them? Of course I had noticed them—they were salient as a fluorescent traffic cone on the freeway—and of course she said them because with her I started with the part and moved to the whole, but the whole is contained within each of its parts, just as the traffic cone, sliced in any direction, produces a curve; just as the cause of my particular illness, and therefore the cause of my encounter with Nothereal, is not to be found in factors of lifestyle or environment but in a flaw in the DNA, an error present in the whole of my body that afternoon in the hospital room when the sun shone brightly for the first time in a few days and Nothereal, for the first time, sat at the side of the bed without saying a word, and I was glad to have her there: an error present as well in each individual cell of my body that afternoon and the afternoon before, and the year before, and ten years before that, when I wandered around Italy, realizing I was in love with two women at the same time, realizing the double bind was in fact inescapable; and ten years before that, in suburban Milwaukee, when my father collapsed from a stroke in the next room and later told me he'd had a vision of Charon telepathically inviting him into the canoe on the river Styx; and ten years before that, when I discovered my parents' hidden collection of books on Picasso and Klee and de Kooning and Mozart records, while, in distant Paris, the Rolling Stones were recording *Some Girls*, an album about New York.

Bone marrow can be extracted directly from the bone, which is highly painful and requires general anesthesia; but much of the same blood-growing material can be removed from the blood itself in basically the same way caffeine can be extracted from coffee (although assumedly the marrow is not subsequently sold to PepsiCo or Coca-Cola). Your veins are hooked up to a vast machine that looks a little like a prop from either *The Elephant Man* or *Dune* (I always think David Lynch really envisioned them as one film), and a centrifugal apparatus starts spinning your blood around until the cells separate according to their weight. The plasma, clear fluid, rises to the top; the red blood cells sink to the bottom; and in the middle rests what they call the "buffy coat," which is, unfortunately, not named after Joss Whedon's delightful vampire-slayer immortalized in the public's eye by the lovely Sarah Michelle Gellar (but portrayed in the original film by Kristy Swanson, thus rendering her the Pete Best of the "Scooby gang"). The buffy coat corresponds to the line of espresso in a latte macchiato; this is where the white and green cells and platelets are trapped, and then grabbed ("harvested") and thrown in the freezer. This procedure can take a few days, although in my case they had enough in about an hour. With the harvest safely in the fridge, the doctor can destroy the body's cells right down to the level of the bone marrow itself, which is where blood cells, necessary for life, are produced. In other words, it allows the doctor to chemo the patient as close as possible to death. The relationship of this high-dose chemo to conventional chemotherapy—which was discovered, in the first place, when medical combat units in the trenches during the First World War noticed that victims of both leukemia and mustard gas had been miraculously cured, and put two and two together—is roughly analogous to that of what Little Boy could do in a moment to the body of Hiroshima in early August of 1945 versus, let's say, what mustard gas could do in a moment of similar duration.

Now there's this relatively narrow window of opportunity when the chemo does its stuff, slaughtering everything in its path like a Mongol army. And just at the last minute, the bone marrow is taken out of the freezer and injected back into the body. This procedure, called engraftment, is almost cartoonish: a special orderly comes in with a huge plastic syringe like something you might see a Tim Burton character wielding; it's semiopaque and full of all your bone marrow; she sticks it in your arm and just pushes it right back in. The cells, like Canadian geese or spermatozoa, intuitively know where to go and, most important, what to do when they get there, which is no simple task: reigniting the production of blood cells, introducing themselves to their new neighbors (i.e., the liver, the heart, the kidneys), and rebooting and organizing the entire immune system.

The only problem with all of this is that sometimes—one in about ten cases—the patient dies. Sometimes from a simple infection, since at this point in the transaction there aren't white blood cells to protect the body from infection. Sometimes the liver can't handle all the stress, throws up her hands, eyes rolling, says to the body, you know what? fuck you, and leaves, slamming the door behind her. Sometimes—in the case of an allogenic, rather than autologous, transplant, when the bone marrow is donated instead of borrowed from the patient's own supply—the new bone marrow mistakes its new host for an alien and commands the immune system to destroy it.

And then sometimes, nobody really knows what the fuck is going on, but the patient's dying anyway. That's what happened to me. I have vague memories of this period, when something started to go wrong. I have to depend on my mother's diary.

> *There is a problem with Joshua having a temperature of*
> *unknown origin. A team of infectious diseases specialty is*
> *summoned by Dr. Q., who says no one has figured out what*
> *underlying bacterial disease is causing the fever. He admits he*

and his staff are stumped. He orders different IV antibiotics and many additional blood-draws.

I remember sensing a change in tone on the part of the staff, and I remember the blood-drawings, the transfusions; but I don't remember feeling that I was actually in real danger. I might not have understood; my memory may be failing; or I might not have been made aware of the situation.

Throughout this period Joshua receives several blood transfusions, day and night. He is supposed to have 3mg of IV Tylenol before each transfusion, but because his platelet counts are in a dangerous state and his hemoglobin level is so low, there is no time to administer the Tylenol. Now the orders are to "transfuse STAT." This is a very serious time for us.

Since he cannot talk, he writes me a note which reads—as well as I can make out his handwriting, because he is in so much pain (and it is in the middle of the night)—

"—what kind of side effects will happen without the 3mg of Tylenol not being used prior to the transfusions?

"—Doesn't the Tylenol reduce the fever?

"—What was I given at ten—what pain killer? I got relief.

"—Should I take . . ." [Unfinished sentence.]

Here, Nothereal first appears in my mother's diary. My mother's transcription of the dialogue between patient, doctor, caretaker, and pain management staff is fascinating in its expression of the fragile complexity in calibrating the collaboration of different specialists.

155

After the next morning rounds with Dr. Q., the pain management team again returns. I notice that a lovely, petite, dark-haired female doctor is part of the group. Another P/M doctor or nurse asks Joshua what his pain level is on a scale of zero to ten. Joshua cannot reply. F. says, "I know you are in a lot of pain, Joshua. Are you at ten?" Joshua then whispers, "No, seven."

The doctor increases the Fentanyl. The conversation continues (some paraphrasing):

JOSHUA: *I am not sleeping. Does the Fentanyl lead to sleep deprivation? I haven't slept for one full hour [i.e., without interruption] in a month.*

F.: *You are not supposed to have hallucinations. They are related to the pain meds. If we get rid of the pain meds, you will have more pain and you will not and cannot get any sleep at all.*

Then F. turned to me.

F.: *[to me] We don't want him sleeping all day and then not at night.*

ME: *What does it matter? The bottom line he needs sleep. He's not going anywhere. Why does it matter when he sleeps?*

F.: *Has he tried the throat lozenges?*

ME: *Obviously, he can't use the lozenges because he cannot swallow.*

F.: *If he needs a rescue every fifteen minutes, then the pain management is not working.*

ME: *Well, I know that. That is why I want more attention brought to pain management. That is why you're here, right?*

F.: *Maybe you're not pressing the rescue button hard enough.*

ME: *Well, here is how I press it. (I get up and walk over to the card and press the rescue button and, of course, it registers.) And, Joshua definitely knows how hard to press the rescue button. Plus I'm with him all the time, and I see when he presses the rescue button. All I know is this (and I look at the entire pain management team): my son is in constant pain and pain management, I've been told, is part of his treatment and recovery. I don't see any decrease in his pain and I want to see some pain management action NOW.*

The lovely, petite, dark-haired female doctor (who, we learn later, is Dr. [Nothereal]) says something to F. about can't she (F.) see the effect Joshua's pain is having not only on him but also his mother who is here 24/7 observing this? The pain management team exits.

Shortly thereafter, the nice nurse-practitioner, A.G., comes in to talk to us. Obviously, she has been told by Dr. [Nothereal] that I had "words" with F., that there are issues between me and the Pain Management team. A.G. is encouraging, pacifying, and compassionate. She assures me that she is "on top of the situation."

My friend Mark had given me his wife Bonnie's sister's daughter's discarded iPod—a little pink Nano obviously more suited for an eight-year-old Asian girl than for me. This fact was funny, and it was also funny that Mark gave it to me without earbuds. Like—gee, thanks. An iPod, with no earbuds. This deeply troubling situation provided my mom the opportunity for a break (she needed one), and so she embarked on a strange odyssey to the Apple flagship store, an odyssey that involved several wrong turns, a memorable encounter with a kindly Madison Avenue doorman, and (really!) a frenzied rickshaw ride down Fifth Avenue during rush hour. When she returned to the hospital, long after sunset,

> Dr. [Nothereal] is alone with Joshua. It is long after her shift, but I am glad Joshua is not alone. She tells me that she would like Joshua to be put on a sedative medication called Haldol instead of Ativan. She also tells me she suspects that Joshua has reached a plateau with the Ativan, that it is no longer helping. She says she has left orders to the nurse to administer Haldol every five hours, but that if it seems like Joshua needs more, I should call the nurse and say "he's worse and more confused," and that he needs another Haldol, even if the five hours has not elapsed. She tells me she has put this into his night order book.

Nothereal at vigil, long after her shift has ended. This I remember; not words, but the feelings, and I'll bet there weren't a lot of words anyway.

Around this point—not a terribly good omen—old friends from college and high school started flying in to the city from all over the country. I was just happy to see them; I didn't really realize why they might have been doing this at this point. Again, we must rely on my mother's record of events.

Joe, a friend of Joshua's from high school, arrives from Chicago to stay for a few days to see Joshua and give me a little relief. Joe is staying at a nearby hotel, but stays each night until about one or two in the morning. He tells us he's going to get another meal and sleep. He will return very early the next morning—which he does. During the course of the day, Joshua has several more vomiting episodes of increasing violence.

    Joe also observes the frequent visits and phone calls from Dr. [Nothereal]. Joe asks me if it looks to me like Dr. [Nothereal] "has a crush" on Joshua. I reply affirmatively. We both smile at each other. We both feel that Joshua is also aware of the extra attention he is receiving from Dr. [Nothereal] but he (Joshua) says out loud that maybe it's just the medication that is influencing his observations or feelings.

    Now very late Saturday night or, perhaps, very early Sunday morning, an emergency chest x-ray is suddenly ordered. Dr. [Nothereal]—who is present as a visitor, not a doctor—and Joe are in the room with me. An x-ray attendant arrives and helps Joshua into a wheelchair. The attendant pushes the chair, I guide the IV cart and Joshua grabs hold of my free hand and says, "Mom, are you coming?" I tell him yes, and that Joe is coming also. Dr. [Nothereal] speaks up and indicates that she is coming as well. As we all get on the elevator to go to radiology, I notice that Dr. [Nothereal] is in tears. Joshua is still holding my hand and he's facing the elevator doors; the wheel-chair fits snugly in the elevator. So Dr. [Nothereal] and Joe are behind him and, therefore, he is not aware of Dr. [Nothereal] crying.

We get off the elevator and are led to the radiology depart-ment. On the walk there, I ask Joe—who has now also seen Dr. [Nothereal] crying—to stay with her and comfort her, as Joshua will not let go of my hand. While Joshua is in radiol-ogy, I wait in the hallway. Finally, I see Joe come around the corner. Dr. [Nothereal] is not with him. I ask him if she's okay. He says that he tried to settle her down as well as he could, that it is a certainty that she has feelings for Joshua that are not just medical concerns, and that she says she doesn't know how I can stay so strong when she, as a person in the medical profession who has become attracted to a patient (which is a forbidden "code" in the medical profes-sion), cannot. She tells Joe that she cannot any longer stand to see Joshua in pain. Joe says he comforted her, tells her that we all appreciate her medical expertise as well as her com-passion. He said she composed herself and said she was going back to her apartment, about a block away from the hospital. Joe had offered to walk her there, but she said it is not necessary. Then Joe and I wait until Joshua is wheeled out of the x-ray room. The attendant, Joe, and I then get Joshua back to his room, all the while Joshua is holding my hand. Joe and I get him back into bed.

Joe is due to leave Monday morning and stops by early that morning before he leaves for the airport. I am so sorry to see

*him leave. He has been so helpful to both Joshua and me. I
wish he could stay.*

*Early Sunday morning, Dr. [Nothereal] visits Joshua again.
He has had another violent night. She checks his medical chart
and says to me, "I ordered no Ativan; I ordered Halydol. The
nurses did not follow my orders." She shows me the medical
chart and her orders. No Halydol was administered throughout the night and she shows me that she ordered haldol IV
.5mg every 8 hours, by the nurse, not on a PRN (as needed)
basis. She also notices that she had ordered no more swish-
and-spit procedures of the mixture of water and lydocain. She
had ordered that the nurse should take a sponge stick, dip it
directly into the pure lydocain and gently swab Joshua's mouth
and tongue that way. This was not indicated as being done in
the record either. She is furious. She exits the room in a fury.*

Then one morning I got up at my normal hour, eight, precisely an hour after rising at my previous normal hour, seven
(the nurses have to wake you every hour, which becomes a
source of vague irritation after a few weeks). I was looking
forward to my morning helping of—well, nothing, actually,
because one of the prime vexations of the transplant is a weird
thing called mucositis, which is when the lining of the mouth
and throat and esophagus is annihilated, so you can't eat or
drink or even swallow; the entire mouth and throat becomes a
plastic white shell that cracks and bleeds even when you're not
vomiting chartreuse bile like Linda Blair or, unlike Linda
Blair, regurgitating horrendous mucus crystals, bizarre coral-

161

sharp glistening black structures that scrape along the unprotected digestive tract, splitting it, before coming out of your mouth and falling to the floor and shattering there. But what I'm describing here is pain, and it is not pain that I felt when I started, that morning, to die.

Of all the things I've set out to describe, this one presents the largest challenge, because the incentive for action—for escape—was not pain. It would be easier to say that it was; in many cases I'm sure it is; but it was not in my case. Not pain even in Nothereal's very broad definition of the word. I've gone through dozens, maybe hundreds of words *à la recherche du bon mot*, and the best I've been able to do, surprisingly, is the oddly neutral "discomfort." But it's the most accurate, I think. What does it mean, normally, to be in discomfort? Let's hypothesize a scenario: you're at a bar, say, when the mediocre techno's a little too loud. Techno's bad enough, and this isn't even good by those standards. The stools are too high, so there's nowhere to anchor your legs, and you feel, faintly, the onset of a muscle cramp. The place is overcrowded; just behind you and to your right, a bunch of people from the DA's office downtown are busy transferring aggression after the week's frustration; their voices purposefully intrude. One woman in particular directs an earsplitting, rueful laugh at your eardrum, all the while taking care to pretend that, as far as she's concerned, you don't exist. The guy with her keeps ordering nauseating cocktails like diet vodka Cokes or Dewar's in 7UP, and the bartender sets 'em up on the sticky bar right in front of you, and a bluesleeved arm continually reaches out an inch from your face to grab them, and each time you wonder if they'll spill on your slacks. You know that in a few minutes you'll have to urinate, but God knows where the bathroom is in this place, and how long the line is. It's slightly too warm inside, too humid; the windows are foggy; there's the slight odor of—well, you know, cheap perfume and sweat and beer and maybe something rotting somewhere. Maybe you're with a couple of friends you don't know too well, and one of them's already been drinking too much, and the other, for some reason, may not like you. But for some reason you're socially obligated to talk with them, although the one guy's talking too quietly for you to possibly make out what he's saying, and the drunk guy's shouting too loud and he's not looking for a response anyway, and you've got another chemo session tomorrow—you know, any bar in New York at six in the evening. And you just want to get out of there. That was the feeling, magnified. You just want to get out of there. But you can walk out of a crowded bar; I couldn't walk out of the hospital. That's the best way I can put it. There are two kinds of people: those who fear death, and those who fear not death but—as Orson Welles noted, not to Merv Griffin two hours before his own death but as a younger man—*age*: a fear they mistake for thanatophobia. It's not nonbeing itself that terrifies them, but wrinkles, the loss of beauty, varicose veins, difficulty walking, general wear-and-tear, forgetfulness, broken hips, the loss of control of one's body, the impossibility of walking, the assisted-living scenario, dementia. But not nonbeing itself. I wonder how the actual approach of the moment of death strikes such people: it might be a surprise. Of course the moment of death isn't a moment at all, but the end of moments, and according to Zeno's paradox of locomotion, in order to get there you must get halfway there, but in order to get halfway there you must get halfway to halfway there, in other words quarterway there, but even in order to get quarterway there you've got to get halfway to quarterway there, which is eighth-way there, and so on. As the morning sun streamed in, my halfway there was a sudden deep ache in my lower back, and my quarterway there was a sudden spike in fever (the worst I've ever experienced and the worst feeling I've ever felt, and it occurred to me why the Christian imagines Hell as hot), and my eighthway there was the ache in my back swirling around to radiate through the torso and then to the arms and the legs and then to the wrists and ankles, then to the fingers and toes and, discovering a barrier to expansion, curling back to the wrists and ankles and hammering spikes into them. Halfway to eighthway I stopped counting because I saw hospital staff rush into the room, and a plethora of tubes shoved into the plethora of UBS-like connectors attached to the catheters in my chest and arms, saw two of Picasso's weeping women, the mother and the lover, Beata Maria Virgo Perdolens and Dora Maar. I was aware that there was much to say to my mother and to Nothe-real. But there was so much other work to be done, and I had such a short amount of time. There was above all else the body, and the need to escape from it; and that need eclipsed all else. Biologists call this escape "death." I realized I had to get out of there, and I told everybody. That if they didn't do something pretty soon, no very soon, no, now, I was leaving. For a person like me who fears death rather than aging, oddly, the experience wasn't, at least in this case, frightening.

(Although death *was* frightening for my father, who was my kind of guy, freaked out by the non-notion of nonbeing. The first time I saw him cry I was around ten; I was sitting on the burnt-orange carpeting of the second living room in the addition we'd built to our house—I can remember when it was still lawn—reading, believe it or not, an art book [this is becoming a recurring motif]. The picture windows looked out onto the back lawn, which was desaturated; it was autumn, afternoon, chilly. He was standing in the middle of the backyard, looking up at the leafless trees; there were crows huddling in the branches, but they weren't calling, they were just sitting there. That was the moment, he said, he knew his mother was dying. He turned around and was crying. His mother was afraid of death, even to the point of asking him if he'd be willing to accompany her. He wasn't willing. She felt betrayed. He felt guilty, betraying her, and also angry at her request. She died. He watched her die. He described the grimace on her face that turned into a smile, and he said from that moment on he had no fear of death. A couple of years later he collapsed in the kitchen; I was in an adjoining room. He'd snapped an incisor in half against a bone in a pork chop, and later he learned that this shock, mercifully perhaps, had triggered a minor aneurysm. Suddenly he wasn't in the kitchen, but was on the banks of the river Styx, facing Charon, whom he described as having a face without features, and who did not speak, although his words were audible, physically; he could have sworn the air molecules were tickling his tympanic membrane. He said he was overwhelmed by an abiding calm, enveloped in warmth. Charon asked him if he wanted to get in the boat. He was a bit afraid to say no for fear of offending the poor boatkeeper, just as he had offended his mother; but he declined nonetheless. That's fine, Charon said. Any time you want. Just know that we're here for you, to take care of you. Now this is what he told me. Did he make all of this up, to reassure me? Or to reassure himself? Because when he really was about to die, he called me up from his place in Oceania, LA, and—opened-mouthed but wordless, unlike Charon, who spoke words with closed mouth—howled like a wild dog.)

But if my experience wasn't frightening, it was—a banal word—sad. There were three things that were sad. There was the external world of, shall we say, appearances, like the appearances of the nurses at the door, the faces of de Kooning's women. But the apparition of these faces seemed to rise slowly to the top of the field of vision: the crown of the heads were cropped, then the foreheads were gone.

Then there was my body, rapidly moving from uninhabitable to unimaginably uninhabitable; therefore taking leave of it was not only not marked by sadness but not entirely without, if not happiness, at least relief. It wasn't exactly the rational wager of taking the chance that what was in store couldn't be worse than this; but it was the recognition that, while not knowing what cards were in that hand that had yet to be turned over, it was now an impossible bet to refuse. In other words, more the feeling of an inevitable flow, a tremendous swell and rise.

Along with the sense of leaving the body was the sense of leaving the mind, feeling it recede. And then there was something new: I first saw it in a flash, but I kept going back to it: a smooth black form, floating in a dark red field, slowly rotating.

What was this thing? Where was it? Each time I saw it, it was easier to discern, as if it were lit by a gradually brightening light source on a dimmer. My mother's face, then this thing, then Nothereal's face, then this thing now slightly better lit than before: still the deepest black I've ever seen, but I could make out a texture on its surface I'd previously held to be as smooth as the surface of undisturbed water, as sheer as a shard of glass cleanly broke. I knew what it was. I recognized it, floating there innocently, suspended. It was the most familiar thing in the world. Funny it was black. When I was around twelve, I'd say, I was surprised to discover, among the thousands of books in my father's library, a book of testimonials of near-death experiences: I was surprised because the book seemed so vulgar. A remarkable number of interviews reported the same thing on the threshold of death: a diffuse white light, an infusion of warmth, an inundating sense of comfort. (A small chapter was given to botched suicides: a remarkable number of subjects reported the overwhelming feeling of having committed a profound breach of metaphysical protocol. Again, how vulgar.) But mine was black, not white. It was there, then my mother was there, then it again, then Nothereal. Like how a movie is edited. Music is the least representational of the arts, and movies are the most. Or are they? Kubrick said once that if one were to compare witnessing a car crash (or some other violent catastrophe visited upon a person, assumedly) to witnessing its representation in any medium, the film version would be the closest to the original; but he also said film adds nothing to the arts that's not already there—except editing, that's unique to the movies and you can't find an analogue to editing in any of the other media. And how we edit our lives. My near-death experience was edited, cutting between the thing slowly rotating and the hospital room; and when I was in grade school, in the classroom, I would easily become bored and restless, particularly in the afternoons, and I would pass the time by "editing" a scene together by employing the six extraocular muscles to switch between the cardinal positions of the gaze, at varying rhythms: between the teacher and the students, say, at different speeds. The teacher's droning monologue wouldn't change, but the difference between staring at her for a whole minute and switching like wildfire between the faces of my comatose classmates—I remember marveling at how this simple choice could change the meaning of what was going on, marveling at how good the actors were, thinking that if a film featured performances this strong and subtle it would be by far the greatest film ever made. The hospital was like this, but not through choice. The views of the black shape were longer in duration now, the views of my mother's face, or Nothereal's, shorter. At first I thought this trend—in music you'd call it a gradual process applied to rhythm—was illusory, a trick of the mind. But no, it was definitely happening. Each time I saw the black shape, it lingered longer than the last, it was closer, and the light source clearly divulged the texture of its surface, not smooth, inscribed, scarred, with traces of being impacted by love, hope, sex, dreams, laughter, joy, loneliness, sex and sex and sex. It wasn't my body and it wasn't my mind, but it bore abrasions from contact with my body and my mind; it was beautiful; it was capable of producing beauty. I beheld it with awe and grief and gratitude. "You're going to be fine," someone said, distantly, in the hospital room. I was seeing less and less of the hospital room. I was losing my body and my mind, and I was approaching this thing—not the body nor the mind—and I wasn't quite ready but there wasn't time to get ready, so I realized I was ready.

I briefly studied ancient Greek, and there's a word in Greek, ψυχή, transliterated into English as "psyche," which has been variously translated, often as "spirit," but what's important is that the word is derived from a verb meaning "to cool, to blow" like a breeze.

I might parenthetically add at this point that there was an unfortunate period in my life and in the life of a woman I loved and who loved me, and we were living together in Paris and were happy and unhappy at the same time, because we loved each other but could not trust each other for reasons too complex to describe here and perhaps elsewhere. We had enjoyed many conversations—in different cities, sometimes in planes, once, while driving across a black bridge, as the sun was sinking—but we had somewhere along the line acquired the unfortunate habit of accidentally, yes, accidentally catching glimpses of each other's notebooks, the ancient Greek equivalent of accidentally, yes, accidentally running across an e-mail or a text message addressed to someone other than oneself. In essence we had designed a perverse epistolary correspondence that ran its course on a stratum parallel to that of verbal communication, and the tension between these strata was seismic in its sudden short shifts and rumblings. One morning when she was in the shower I glimpsed a phrase in her lovely, smooth as sandalwood penmanship:

—*The wind of the senses*

O what gorgeous minds we had. I was sleeping with someone she knew and she was sleeping with a friend of mine, and I realized with a start that she was quoting me, quoting a phrase she had accidentally glimpsed in one of my notebooks I had accidentally left open like a mouth that opens in order to cry out. She had quoted me out of rue and spite and above all envy. But in her haste and, I'm certain, fear of being discovered, she'd gotten the quote wrong. What I had written (emphasis mine [I mean it's mine now, it wasn't there then]) was,

—*The wind* beneath *the senses*

which isn't better, just different—but for our purposes, more apt. For this is what I saw: the black form of the cooling ψυχή, the breath of the wind beneath the senses.

Meanwhile, the hospital staff was trying to save my life. My mother's record:

I am horrified when Dr. Q. says to Joshua, in a rather demanding/threatening/curt tone, "What day is it today?" (I didn't even know what day it was!) Joshua replies, Wednesday. In fact, it's early Thursday. Then Dr. Q. continues, in this matter-of-fact tone: "Who is the President of the United States?" Joshua just looks at him in a confused state. As do I. He says to the doctor, "I don't think I can answer any more questions right now. Could we do this on another day?" He begins to cry.

I'm holding my tongue, but furious that Joshua is being subjected to some kind of interrogation. And all of these "white coats" surrounding him. It is very intimidating. And I look at Joshua and he looks just like my husband. It is a moment of some kind of special "out-of-body" experience, this father-son relationship, and I am shaken by it. I begin to cry. I am "seeing" my husband and know he suffered when he died. I am overwhelmed by emotion, confusion, by—I don't know what. I started to cry. A young nurse sees me and tries to comfort me and I am angry and cannot be comforted. I tell her to leave me alone, which she does, reluctantly. My heart is breaking over so many things: Joshua's pain, his being hit by this obscene disease, his incredible courage in being a good and cooperative patient, in his tolerating a situation which never should have happened to this beautiful and good young man, the medications which do not seem to be helping . . . so many things. All I know is that I am furious with God.

And apparently I was calling out for my father. And I don't
remember saying this, but I said to my mother,

—Oh, this is the last place I'll ever see.

It's interesting that I used the word "place." I was referring
to the hospital room. But I remember thinking that the hospital room—the place—was not the last *thing* I would ever see. I
remember the hospital room disappearing, and then I was
alone with the beautiful, beckoning, softly curved, black
ψυχή within the red field. It was very close now. There were
rivulets, webs of parched canals, that reflected the light like
insect wings. A Babylonian stele, the underside of a beetle or
scarab. Nothing viewed from such proximity could possibly be
smooth. And there was no doubt that its slow, pulsating rhythm
had been perfectly timed, perfectly leading up to this moment,
like Debussy's use of time, the perfection of that. I couldn't see
my mother and I couldn't see Nothereal, but they could see me,
and here's the very real sense in which regarding the suffering
of others is worse than experiencing one's own suffering; it
was I who was spared seeing them.

•

THEN ONE OF the millions of random meds they'd been
pumping into my body this whole time kicked in, and I was
back in the hospital room feeling pretty much fine—horrible
but normal horrible, not incomprehensibly unendurably

horrible—and Nothereal's stunning beauty was tearstudded, crying in relief. I think I was too. That was the moment I knew I'd make it through, and I didn't think about the ψυχή for a good long while; there must be some mechanism that kicks in, at that point, so that you don't think about the ψυχή, for a good long while.

I did not want to die: I still don't want to die: I did *not* like not yet having been born.

•

A MERE FEW pages later into my mother's journal we find this:

> *Josh says "something feels very positive"*

•

(LATER MY MOTHER would write:

> *I tell Dr. Q. that I was unkind to the young nurse who tried to comfort me in the foyer, that I need to see her, to apologize to her. He finds her for me. I ask her to forgive me. I hug her. I cry, and I tell her I hope she never, once she has children, ever has to see her child so sick. She is sweet and lovely, tells me she understands, tells me she will check in on us all day long (which she does). I tell her I am lucky to have her with us. I say to her, "forgive me.")*

·

IN THE HOSPITAL, I began to feel better so gradually that I couldn't even tell I was feeling better until, one day, I realized I was bored; and this was an important realization, because in order to feel boredom you must be feeling better than I had been feeling before. Feeling well enough and bored enough to ask to see a music therapist, which was funny; well enough and bored enough to ask to see the priest in residence, the imam in residence, the rabbi in residence. Apparently they were in high demand, because I was only able to see the rabbi. The conversation was brief. He seemed a little distracted. I asked him about death: what if this is all there is? And he said,

You mean, if this is it, then this is it?

I said, Yes, exactly. What if this is it?

He said, nodding, Well, if this is it, then this is it.

And then he looked at me, smiled, shook my hand, and said he had another patient to see.

·

THE RELEASE WAS sudden, and we were unprepared. It was a sunny morning, and suddenly the staff appeared and announced that I was free to leave. I called my friend Drew—he's an old friend of mine, a Vietnam vet, a wonderful writer who has his own stories to tell, some of which are not entirely unlike mine—and he drove over and picked us up, my mother and me. We walked outside into sunlight and real air, outside air, and I felt as if I'd never been outside. Then into the car and, setting keel to breakers, went forth on godly York, with its more trucks and its less cabs as it pushed the city toward its limits and pointed beyond them; then on the pale ribbon of the FDR, boring us outward, through that peculiar, seemingly sourceless, greenish blue light of midtown, the light reflected many times over off the glass of skyscrapers, like it's been spun in a centrifuge; past the 59th Street Bridge, the least elegant, most aggressively, heavily industrial of our bridges, not a joiner, but an exit, pointing elsewhere; along the river, under concrete pedestrian overpasses that connect hospitals to schools; past the sharply soft green jewel of the United Nations building, so lonely and lovely alone against the raging sea of the East River, like helpless Andromeda; the water was beautiful and black, and the traffic was deafening. Timing has been so important in this account: the day of my release happened to coincide with the last page of the little diary my mother was keeping.

The sentence is written on the top half of the last sheet of the ruled notebook. It occupies five of the total thirty lines of the page. These five lines are not consecutive. The first two are separated from the last three by an empty line.

The sentence does not end with a period or any other mark of punctuation.

It is encircled.

•

WHEN I WAS a kid, my mom used to take me to this old diner on North Avenue, Ted's, for a hamburger and a shake, as if we were in the 1950s. At a certain point I felt as if I were outgrowing it.

when Drew picked us
up to take us home,

Josh said, with
relief,
"I love traffic"

(Immaturity!) One of the last times we had lunch there, I'd by then discovered music, discovered the immensity of it. We always sat at the counter. On the wall facing us hung a print of a painting. I don't recall anything about the painting except that it was bad. (I want to remember it as one of those postwar American geometric abstracts by a forgotten mediocrity—a babyblue, cottoncandy fuzzball lanced by a brown vector against an orange field—but I'm probably making that up.) We were looking at it, and I said to my mom, "No wonder painting is more accessible to the public than music; with music you have to wait for time to get the form, but with painting it's all immediately there."

"Sure," she said. "I mean look how off that thing is, most people would have some intuitive sense, even if they couldn't explain it, that—" and here she described the awkwardness of the composition.

I don't remember saying "I love traffic" as we left the hospital. Obviously I did. These were, then, among the last of a whole series of words I don't remember saying. I don't know how many words I said that I've forgotten, and I don't know how many of those were recorded. The idea about the difference between perceiving form in music and painting was the type of thing I'd talk about more often with my father than with my mother. I think that by the time my mother and I were having lunch at Ted's that afternoon, I'd realized they were separating. I was in college by then. We were sitting next to each other, she to my right, and she was framed by a window; her posture was slightly straighter than normal; North Avenue was outside. It occurs to me now that one reason I mentioned the possible difference between perceiving music and painting was that I'd realized they were separating.

Pretty soon after that I went to Europe for a few months. I remember my parents waving goodbye, at the airport. It was the last time I saw them together.

My dad told me once—"You know your mother can't listen to serious music like Bach anymore. It's too overwhelming. That's why she listens to light music, when she listens at all."

When I returned to college after that trip to Europe my parents would visit me separately, I'd visit them separately. One afternoon my dad dropped by. At the time, I had fallen in love with Mahler and was infatuated with a movement from his third symphony, a slow, *misterioso* setting of Nietzsche's "Midnight Song." I played it for my dad. He said, "My God, how sad."

Not too long after that my mom came by. I never knew exactly where they were in their breakup, and I never asked. I put on a beautiful recording of the slow movement of Mahler's sixth symphony. It was played by the Chicago Symphony Orchestra, and my teacher was on the CD. After a minute she said, "I'm sorry, I have to ask you to turn that off."

One morning not too long after that, my father awoke early, got in his car, and drove to the Arizona desert. He rented an apartment and wrote voraciously. He hadn't written in many years. He had been creatively inactive during those years; he'd been busy raising a family, working in radio and television and advertising, reading when he could, lots of poetry, Anglo-Saxon, Native American, the Greeks. He would eventually reconcile with my mother, but he would never see her again.

The first time I saw my mother in tears was the morning after John Lennon had died in New York. She was driving me to grade school. I was too young to know who he was, but I had the sense that he was of some importance.

One of the final songs Lennon wrote before he died is called "Watching the Wheels." It's a poetic defense of artistic inaction. For about five years, Lennon wrote no music. He was busy raising his son, spending time with his wife, reading Plato. During this time, as he says in the song, "people" (which means "the self") had been calling him lazy; people had been wondering if he was okay just "watching the shadows on the wall." I'm fine, he replies, in the song, just sitting here watching the wheels go around.

My father ended up living in L.A., and he'd get sick and get better and get sick and get better. One time he called and I happened to be sitting at my computer, and something impelled me to start typing. I had never recorded his words before. He was in a good mood. "I'm just sitting on the edges of the ends of life," he said, "feeling no pressure to do anything."

It turned out to be our last conversation (a talk from which I shall draw later in this essay). Odd that I'd had the impulse to transcribe it. Odd that I recorded the last things he ever said to me. The song "Watching the Wheels" features a dulcimer, the Hungarian instrument in the basement restaurant where I never celebrated my entrance into the Liszt Academy in 1933. That dream is over. Before Mr. Lennon's dulcimer song was released, a young man, holding a book, fired hollow-point bullets through his body, and he lost 80 percent of his blood, and died. It was announced on the news: one guy standing outside the Dakota told the newscaster, ominously, that "the eighties have begun." The next morning my mother was driving me to grade school and it was the first time I'd seen her cry. Exactly 9,683 days later I left the hospital. It takes about eight minutes to get from Mr. Lennon's apartment to the hospital I was watching, from my vantage point in the car, recede, watching the traffic, which I evidently loved. You pull out of the garage and drive east on West Seventy-Second Street, take the first right, onto Central Park West; cross the park (you'll use the Sixty-Fifth Street Transverse, as they call it, but don't worry about what it's called, just take the second left), continue through the park until you get to East Sixty-Fifth Street, keep going, then turn left on York: your destination will be on your left. To get from the hospital to the apartment, simply reverse the steps. There was no public service for Mr. Lennon, nor was there for my father.

The original draft of "Watching the Wheels" was entitled "I'm Crazy" and contains lyrics that were dropped, modified, exchanged. For example, in the final version Mr. Lennon writes of how he's happy just sitting there, how he loves to watch the wheels "roll," a word that's then half-rhymed, in an assonant slant, with "go."

But in the original version, he loves, instead, "the traffic flow": a perfect rhyme that was thus discarded before it was released, and therefore—like all excisions before release, for better or worse—is known and missed by only a precious few.

VII

A SERIES OF VIGNETTES,
WHICH TURN TO MELODRAMA

Diffused over her face was the dark pallor which I adore . . .
Upon her mouth was the glorious, cruel smile which the
divine Leonardo pursued in his paintings. This smile was
in sad combat with the sweetness of the long eyes.

—*Gabriele d'Annunzio*, "Gorgon"

It wasn't until a comment made much later by my
oncologist—"You had a difficult hospitalization!"—that I realized I'd nearly died. It was after I'd had my first outing with
Nothereal; I believe it was she who invited me, but we had been
corresponding since I'd been convalescing at home, first by
letter (beautifully old-fashioned, gracious, I thought), then by
e-mail and phone. Finally, we went to a Romanian film at the
Film Forum called *12:08 East of Bucharest* (unfortunate English
translation), which had recently won pretty big at Cannes.
Romania was, and is, at this time of writing, enjoying a flush of
activity in film that might well be seen someday as a golden

age, along the lines of Australian or Hong Kong cinema of the 1970s and '80s. It's a film about a host of a local talk show in a small town in the north of Romania. He's trying to broadcast a roundtable discussion on the Romanian revolution, which occurred sixteen years to the day before. Gradually the film reveals ambiguity on the parts of the characters' testimonials: did they commit themselves to the revolution before victory was assured, or did they wait until Ceauşescu was forced to flee the capital by helicopter? The gravity of this investigation into truth, guilt, and self-delusion is counterpointed by the ineptitude of the small television studio's technical crew: the director of the film, Corneliu Porumboiu, presents the last act of his story as the telecast itself. During one character's impassioned defense of his actions (or inactions) on the night in question, the camera almost imperceptibly pans down, so his face seems to rise slowly to the top of the frame: the crown of his head is cropped, then his forehead is gone, but it's like watching the sun set; one doesn't see the actual movement, only its result. At this point, the viewer's reminded that the small station lacks the funds to replace a faulty camera tripod. I enjoyed the movie, and it brought my trips to Eastern Europe back to me. But Nothereal, Serbian, seemed bored. Was I just a tourist? I wondered about that. Remember that everything the traveler sees, the foreigner sees, seems quintessentially x, x representing the adjectival form of the place within which stands the traveler. You're sitting in Belgrade, for instance, in some random café. A few guys come in wearing suits; they're murmuring to each other, deciding what to order, or where to sit.

You watch their every move, their every gesture, every nuance. How quintessentially Romanian they are! To your right, there's a fluorescent-lit refrigerated beverage display case stocked with Pellegrino, fruit juice, Coke, and some type of locally produced energy drink. Look at how the bottles and cans are arranged! Look at the way that woman drinks her frozen latte, hunched over, sipping through a straw: look at the way she's peering around, birdlike. The way she's peering around, birdlike, how uniquely, quintessentially Serbian!

But how many hundreds or thousands or millions of exact replicas of this exact gesture of this exact woman are being performed at exactly that moment, in Guadalajara? in Azerbaijan? in Prague? in New York?

But put the frame of Serbia around this girl, sitting there across from you, in the café, at four o'clock in the afternoon, sunnier now than before, the day's turned surprisingly warm, and she's unique.

On the other hand, is it entirely arbitrary to ascribe something that might be called communal trauma to a country whose government rounded up some thirty thousand people—men, women, children, infants—and began executing the men and not only the men, and began raping the women and not only the women. The crowning achievement in postwar mass murder occurred at the same time that, a mere thousand miles away, the classically trained musician Alan Wilder made the heartbreaking announcement of his departure from celebrated synth-pop band Depeche Mode. I remember when the survivors' testimonials began to circulate. A boy was asked to rape his sister and, upon refusing, was murdered. A mother's child beheaded while sitting on her lap. Members of the sequestered choosing suicide. I was traumatized by these stories, but I was worlds away, in Paris. What if I had been in Belgrade, in Bosnia? What if the trauma had been more direct? How would such events affect the very citizens of the nation that committed such acts? I'd fallen victim—directly—to the trauma of a life-threatening illness, a life-threatening treatment, the experience of almost dying: didn't I go a little mad?

I distinctly remember waiting for her before the movie, on the corner of Sixth Avenue and Houston, and seeing her across the river of traffic and feeling so unsteady—I was still unused to walking—that I wondered if I'd be able to cross the street to meet her. After all, nothing had actually *happened* between us when I was in the hospital. I wasn't sure even now if there would be anything between us. I indistinctly remember her wearing a red dress, so that she resembled a cardinal, not a crow, on a black branch against a white sky, but that may be a false ascription. I distinctly remember waiting in line at the movie theater and talking about exercise, and her smile as she said that she liked yoga because it improved her orgasms. I indistinctly remember my reaction to this. I think I vaguely wondered if Nothereal had read and taken the advice of Madonna, who, in her 1992 book *Sex*, explains to the reader that "on every date you have to say one really disarming thing."[15] I distinctly remember the feeling of sitting next to her, in the movie theater, the feeling of watching two movies at the same time, in one of which I was a participant: the feeling that she felt this too.

The movie was presented by the Romanian Cultural

Center—the foreign branch of the Ministry of Culture—and there was a random lottery for a DVD of another film by the director: a random ticket receipt was chosen; and I knew we would win, and we did.

Then there was a single glass of wine somewhere nearby the cinema, either before or after the movie, and she looked at me, apropos of nothing and everything, and said,

—if you have to go back in the hospital I won't be able
to help you now.

Her voice was low, and she was not smiling. She looked down, and up again.

This was her lovely professionalism. Nothing had happened, nothing had been breached, when I was in the hospital, when she was a member of my staff.

At some point soon thereafter I went to her apartment, ostensibly to make the acquaintance of her cat. She had an austere, almost clinical flat a block from the hospital; there was something elegantly minimalist about it, but also something of the anonymity of the Eastern Bloc, the big grey shoeboxes just outside of Prague or Budapest. She had very few books, half a dozen, maybe. The place was spotless—hospital spotless. There was a couch and there was a single chair for her desk, and we looked at the couch and then the chair and then at each other. Do you want to take a walk? she said.

We walked along the river, which is, in that strange upper-east corner of the city, also to walk along a highway, and to walk under concrete pedestrian overpasses that connect various buildings of hospitals and medical schools. The water was beautiful and black, and the traffic was deafening, and other than that, there was only concrete, like what they thought, in the 1960s, things would look like now. At this point we weren't saying too much.

We went back to her apartment. I moved the single chair to the middle of the bare room and sat down. She sat down in front of me, and I touched and then pulled her hair so that her head bent back. Then our bodies were pure as black water and as austere as concrete, as tight as the surface of black water.

So what were the signs, and when did they occur? In what order, what frequency? Was it she who revealed them, gradually, like a stripper revealing, and disassociating, parts of the body; or was it I, as my senses and my body and my mind gradually came back to life, who noticed them, one by one, part by part, reassembling the parts into a whole? We were in a café one morning, and she visibly tensed up, her almost almond eyes narrowing. A couple of good-looking TriBeCa guys had walked in; I had already vaguely recognized, without giving it any thought, that they were gay. She wanted to leave. So there

were those kinds of things. One time we were walking down Canal Street, and we passed a trio of Hasidim, and she clenched my hand. We were having dinner outside at the Odeon one night and a friend of mine walked by. He lives in the neighborhood; he's a television producer; he's Jewish. I introduced him to Nothereal. I have no idea what transpired during the fraction of the second in which they exchanged glances, but he bid us goodnight and before he was half a block away I received a text message from him. It read

don't walk run

At the same time, one night she came over to my apartment, crying, because she had met a new patient earlier that afternoon who was about to undergo a bone marrow transplant; she, thinking of me, could barely talk to him.

At the same time, she e-mailed me a research article about survival rates for patients in my situation. There were lots of variables, but as far as I could tell, the findings put my chances at 13 percent. This was, in a word, disappointing.

I printed the article out and showed it to my oncologist. "Hell is this?" he said. He scanned it, frowning. Then he was furious. "Who gave this to you?"

Of course I couldn't say—your colleague, who is treating your patients; your colleague, with whom I'm sleeping. "I found it online."

"Look at this," he muttered. He was referring to the authors of the article, their credentials, the footnotes, their sources. "Bunch of amateurs. Listen to me. Don't go online with this stuff. Promise me that. If you have questions, ask."

And at the same time, the sex with her was more and more frequent, more and more frantic, more and more thrilling and impulsive, and then—compulsive? As were the adamant declarations of love. I chalked it up to the infatuation that I felt as well, my infatuation with her salt-bright beauty. But I also noticed that, increasingly, I was defending myself against vague accusations. Apologizing for not calling her right back. She's vulnerable, I thought. But how vulnerable—vulnerable to the point of berating me for not calling her back within an hour? She said she was terrified when I wasn't with her. That when I wasn't there, it was as if I didn't exist, as if an object in a room, temporarily obscured by someone standing in front of you, has disappeared. One morning I told her I was having a business meeting with an old friend, an author, a woman, and Nothereal said our relationship was over, that there was no way she deserved to be treated with such contempt. I apologized: I said I should have—what? I can't remember what I said. Something about telling her things earlier, not springing things on her, I have no idea.

But the worst were the stares. Once, again at the movies, I felt the smarting sensation of burning on my cheek, and realized she'd been staring not at the screen but, fixatedly, at me. For how long? And then there was the time we were walking back to my apartment, and she was doing the same thing. (The French have a word for staring someone down, *devisager*, literally "de-facing.") I looked at her, smiled, looked back ahead, looked back at her, puzzled. "This isn't going to work," she said.

"What?"

"I just don't have to settle for someone who treats me this way. I deserve more."

We'd reached my apartment. I was preoccupied by the results of the first big post-transplant CT scan, which were coming in a few days. If the scan was clean, that boded pretty well. Sara's hadn't been. She was a fellow patient I'd met in the hospital. Her story was pretty much the same as mine: she had the same thing I had, chemo didn't work, so they did the same thing. But in her case the transplant didn't work either. The first post-transplant scan was positive. They gave her six months, and she'd died in three. Nothereal was aware of this.

"You deserve more? Seek more, then," I shrugged, and left her on the corner, alone; I didn't look back, but just before I turned away, I'd caught the expression of incredulousness on her face.

She called the next day, had to see me. She came over. I'm in love with you, she said. Sometimes I go a little off.

"What do you mean?" I asked.

"Sometimes I go a little off. I need you to pull me back, like how you did last night. I need you."

There was the sound of gentle rain in her voice, and our bodies were water again, that night, and the next night, at her apartment; there were defiant, tear-studded cries of love, dreams of children, voiced aloud; never felt anything like this ever never ever and she said she felt she was tipping over into something. I could feel her amber skin move over her skeleton; I wondered if it were our skeletons that were making love. Ever never ever.

I slept late the next morning, over at her place; she went to work. My phone rang: it was my brother, Matthew, who is three years my junior; he had moved to New York from Los

Angeles after the death of our father in 2001. Like me, he was fooling around in the arts; he had studied music and had conducted concerts; he was an excellent conductor. Lately he'd been trying his hand at acting. He was calling to ask whether Nothereal and I would consider being extras in a student film he was involved with. The scene was to take place in a restaurant; there had to be diners dining in the restaurant for verisimilitude's sake. It would be filmed in a couple of days, the night before I was to receive my scan results. I thought it might be fun, a distraction. I told him I'd ask Nothereal. I called her up and asked her if she was into the idea of sitting in a restaurant for a couple of hours, pretending to eat. She said sure.

I got to the restaurant first. She was late. She walked into the restaurant with an uncanny smile. Not her smile. Her gaze was steady, direct, preternatural. I already felt blood draining from my face. She wouldn't speak. I asked her how she was. Silence. Just a smile. I tried engaging her in conversation. Silence.

Finally she spoke, an odd relish in her voice. She told me she had to be honest. She hated to tell me this now, because she knew I was worried about the results of the scan tomorrow, and how Sara's results had been, in the oncologist's words, "disappointing," and how he'd given her six months to live and she died in three, and her lover had gone mad and was committed to a psychiatric hospital. But, Nothereal said, she just couldn't keep the façade alive any longer. She felt I had to know the truth: that she didn't love me, that she didn't even like me; that frankly she could hardly bear the sight of me, it was so depressing. I started literally shaking. It crossed my mind that tomorrow I might be dead in three months.

"What's the matter?" she asked.

"I don't believe you," I said.

She went on. She had been lying to me about her love for the past few months out of pity, she said; but she couldn't continue the lies. It was unfair to me, and, most of all, it was unfair to her; she deserved better than this.

"Why are you saying this?" I asked. "Because if you continue, you realize, I'm going to walk out of here and never see you again, and I'm just not sure if that's what you want."

But it has to be this way, she said. Her face was immune, angelic, her eyelashes sympathetic and mocking, her chin defiant. "The disease came for a reason," she said, "haven't you realized that?"

"I'm not sure what you mean."

Staring into my eyes from a thousand miles away, she said,

—But surely you know, deep down, why you're diseased.

She was one of my doctors. I stared back for a few moments, and then I got up and left.

She followed me outside, for reasons unclear to me. The street was busy; the sun was setting. She was laughing delightedly. She ran after me, touched me. "Don't touch me," I said. She laughed again, playfully, and tagged me, like a child on the playground.

I whipped around and screamed so loudly my throat went raw.

Get the fuck away from me!

Everybody on the street, all the extras, turned around on cue, and now her face was the slick wall of a tsunami before its glassy crash.

I walked away briskly. Six blocks later, I received a text from Nothereal. It read, simply:

Loser!

What happened then? Ah, let's see. I ran into a bar and ordered a whiskey. I called a friend who lived nearby, told him what had happened. He came over right away. He didn't understand it either. "Not only that but she's your doctor!" After another drink, I felt a little calmer. We went to the restaurant next door. We happened to be seated next to Chelsea Clinton's table; she's the daughter of a woman who, once, was one of my adopted state's senators who, like me, had adopted it, and who, like me, has since moved on to bigger and better things; and Chelsea's also the daughter of one of my country's former presidents. She was with three others; she seemed like an extremely nice girl, and in person was very attractive. My friend and I enjoyed a good meal. I had trout.

My friend got up to go to the bathroom. Suddenly, alone, I was seized with terror. I rose and ran out of the restaurant. And I mean ran. Chelsea Clinton was like what the fuck. I ran blocks, I don't know how many blocks. I ran into another bar.

My heart was pounding, of course. I ordered another whiskey, called another friend who lived nearby. (The nice thing about living in a small town like New York is that no matter where you are, you're always about two blocks from somebody's place.) I tried to explain what had happened; he came over, found the whole situation as strange as I did.

Finally, I'd calmed down. I walked back to my apartment, relaxed. I got inside and closed the door. Then I was alone again. There was no sound. I switched on a beautiful old glass lamp—Oriental, deep bourbon—I'd inherited from my father. There was still no sound.

It was about two in the morning. Scan results in eight hours. I sat down to write in my journal. That's what my father's advice always was: write it out, write it out. I started to describe a film I was thinking of making. Some notes about lighting: diffused light for the wide shots, conversations (over the shoulder) use direct keys with high contrast. And then a note about the form: a series of vignettes, which turn to melodrama.

Diffused light for the wide shots
Conversations (over the shoulder) use direct keys with high contrast
This is exactly what we are doing
A series of vignettes, which turn to melodrama

But why would Nothereal have done that, if it wasn't that she knew the transplant had failed, and, in love, made the break in a somewhat psychotic but, given the circumstances, somewhat understandable way? They already had the results. They'd had them for days. And Nothereal obviously had access. She'd looked already—How could she not look? How could she resist looking? Like Orpheus and Eurydice. Of course he'd look back—are you coming back up with me, or not?

This thought unsettled me—so I put on some music. The Stones. But now the dreadful rising crest had begun.

Diffused light for the bird shots
Conversations (over the shoulder) use direct rays with high contrast
This is exactly what we are doing
A series of vignettes, which turn to melodrama
_____
Listening to the Rolling Stones and reghas. Raging and
At what?

It hadn't worked for Sara so why would it work for me. Sara—same diagnosis, same chemo, same not working, same salvage treatment, didn't work. Sara—same thing, she was a month ahead of me, that's all, I'd been following her from behind, like the second voice of a two-voice fugue: same thing, just a delay in time.

But there's no reason to think that. Am I losing my mind? Write it out, write it out. Just keep pen to paper: I am trying very hard:

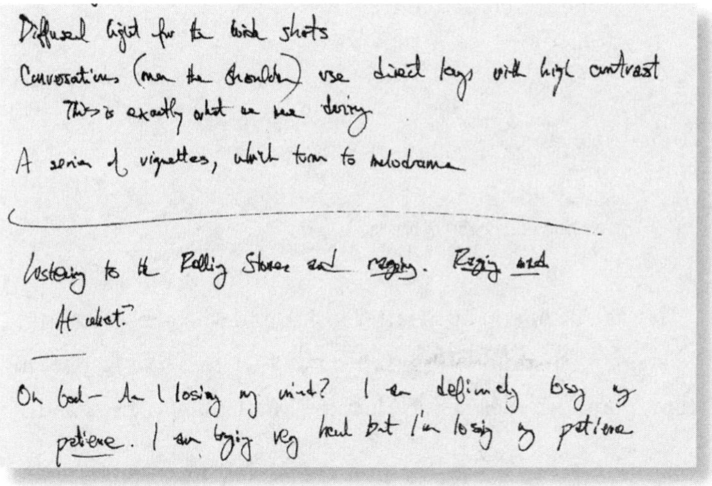

[handwritten note]

Diffused light for the wide shots

Conversations (more the shoulder) use direct keys with high contrast

This is exactly what we are doing.

A series of vignettes, which turn to melodrama

Listening to the Rolling Stones and raging. Raging and

At what?

Oh God— Am I losing my mind? I am definitely busy my patience. I am trying very hard but I'm losing my patience

Ezra Pound spent most of his life working on a long poem called *The Cantos*. He told Yeats that when it was finished (he never finished it) the form would be "like that of a Bach fugue"—"no plot, no chronicle of events, no logic of discourse."[16] (Sorry to cut in for a second — but to a musician this makes absolutely no sense whatsoever. But that's okay; he knew nothing about music; he was responsible for the revival of Vivaldi, for heaven's sake, which might well have aided his insanity plea.) The poem was fragmentary. In the hospital, he wrote a note that wasn't used in the poem but was in its style.

> *Problem now is*
> *not to go stark*
> *screaming hysteric . . .*

And later

young doctors absolutely
useless.

And a little later

grey mist barrier impassible [sic][17]

It wasn't a poem, but a letter to a friend who consoled him. I was alone. "I could *kill* myself now," I write, "like Jason," my roommate, "in these horrible rages and I am being so good":

> Diffused light for the birth shots
> Conversations (over the shoulder) use direct lays with high contrast
>   This is exactly what we are doing
> A series of vignettes, which turn to melodrama
>
> _____
>
> Listening to the Rolling Stones and raging. Raging and
> At what.
>
> Oh God — Am I losing my mind? I am definitely losing my
> patience. I am trying very hard but I'm losing my patience
>
> Rages — I could kill myself, like Jason, in these terrible rages
>   and I am being so good — trying so hard — with no
>   one listening
> And it's a goddamned nightmare of anxiety and adrenaline.

But it's just a goddamned nightmare of anxiety and adrenaline. That's all.

But in a fugue, one voice follows another at some preordained delay. They gave Sara six months. She had her transplant before I had mine. But no—they gave Carmilla six months three or four or five or howevermany times and she's fine— she's drinking martinis and smoking cigarettes and sharing wonderful moments with people including me. So why am I not in a fugue with Carmilla? But why *wouldn't* I be in a fugue with Sara? Because Nothereal knows I'm in the fugue with Sara, not with Carmilla, because she checked the records, and that's why she left. And the *Cantos* was a fugue, and a guy who knows, Noel Stock, the critic, a very smart guy, said that "the *Cantos* is a tragedy."[18] But they gave Sara six months and there, the organs of her body stopped functioning, one by one. Three months in, she was having a tough morning. She was at home, in bed with her lover—she was a lesbian—and she started vomiting blood. Her lover called the hospital, called 911, called the ambulance, but Sara, who was supine, didn't seem to care about any of that: she was shouting "I'm not dying, I'm not dying—I can get up, watch, I can get up by myself." And of course she couldn't. And her lover knew the ambulance wouldn't get there in time. Sara looked at her and between pukes of blood repeated—I can get up by myself. But Carmilla is okay; but Carmilla cast her breasts, her torso, in plaster, and hung it on the wall. Sara's lover bent down and kissed Sara and placed her hands around her lower back, and gently lifted her upright, lifted the torso upright like the torso of a Greek statue might not be the original, it might have been from another one originally and later, in Rome, upon this one, that faces you, affixed—and gently lifted her upright and Sara laughed and smiled and said—see I told you I'm not dying, I told you I could sit up by myself, and her lover nodded, yes, you did sit up by yourself, you're not dying, and Sara's eyes rolled up: the top of the iris was eclipsed, then half the pupil, like the apparition of the sun setting upon a rim of water, but inverted, the water meeting the edge of the sky from above, which would make no sense, then the whole pupil, now the sun is down/up but there's still light, but then the rest of the iris, black and gold and shimmering like an insect's wing, copper and wine and the rest of the iris was eclipsed and she died. And now, later, her lover is a patient in a psychiatric ward just like Ezra Pound was, writing his fugues, and Yeats described the writing as

> constantly interrupted, broken, twisted into nothing
> by its direct opposite, nervous obsession, nightmare,
> stammering confusion . . . This loss of self-control,
> common among uneducated revolutionists, is rare—
> Shelley had it in some degree—among men of Ezra
> Pound's culture and erudition.[19]

Whoops and here's the break:

Diffused light for the birth shots
Conversations (over the shoulder) use direct rays with high contrast
   This is exactly what we see during
A series of vignettes, which turn to melodrama

Listening to the Rolling Stones and raging. Raging and
   At what?

Oh God— Am I losing my mind? I am definitely busy my
   patience. I am trying very hard but I'm losing my patience

Rages— I could tell myself, like Jesus, in these terrible rages
   and I am being so good — trying so hard — with no
   one listening
And it's a goddamn mixture of anxiety and adrenaline.

There it is—the loss of language, the reversion to the purely
graphic, like the cavemen painting under torchlight at Las-
caux. Mr. Tytell writes of Pound, arrested for treason, in the
six-foot-by-six-foot "gorilla" cage, open to the elements, for
three weeks, soldiers staring at him but no one speaking: then
the breakdown.

In later years he characterized the experience by saying, "The World fell in on me." Actually, the breakdown was a wordless catharsis . . . Hemingway had once told him that a writer needed to feel terrific pain before releasing his subject. The breakdown was an admission of such pain. Pound, the man of words, was now caught in the most overwhelming moment of his life without the power to summon language.[20]

Although if I do say myself, my breakdown was not accomplished without some relish of artistry. Let's zoom in on a detail of my inadvertent contribution to Abstract Expressionism in America.

Because what in the name of God is the sense of any of this at all. And I'm alone, without Nothereal, without anyone, and Nothereal is not in a psychiatric ward, because she has access to my records. Wretched outcast, deprived of my kinsmen. There was no sound. The beautiful old glass lamp—Oriental, deep bourbon—I'd inherited from my father. There was still no sound. I picked the lamp up and hurled it against the wall with two arms. Its trajectory was straight, not a curve. The end of the trajectory made sound. I went into the kitchen, got a glass from the cupboard, and filled it with water, and drank. Then I threw the glass against the wall. Then I picked up every glass in the cupboard and threw each one against the wall, glass by glass, until there were no more glasses. Then I picked up a plate and threw the plate against the wall. Then I threw every plate in the cupboard against the wall. I had a nice coffee table from India, a heavy glass top set into a rosewood frame. I picked up the heavy glass and I didn't throw it against the wall; I flung it across the room, so it made an arc, and it landed on the floor, and the sound of this green glass cracking wasn't tinny and trebly like the plates and glasses had been; this was deep and resounding, so now things are getting serious, like listening to the original recordings remastered, like the original recordings were good enough to merit remasterings.

I have a set of four matching antique Chinese chairs. They're hand-carved, out of teak, and even the plates that are set into the backs of the chairs—sculpted reliefs of scenes from Peking opera—would be valuable if sold as parts, apart from the wholes to which they belong. I paid far too much money for them, thousands of dollars, but even so I got them at a bargain (I'd wanted to treat myself on moving to New York). They're quite heavy; by the time I had lifted the last one over my head and smashed it directly down into the wood floor, shattering it, I was tired. I walked over to the destroyed coffee table, glass and wood crunching under my feet like forest leaves and twigs.

The table's thick green glass had broken into big, sharp hunks, and I picked one up. I felt the sudden need to squeeze something, the need for release—what biologists call "escape." I did that, and then I looked down at my hand, which was bleeding freely. I squeezed tighter. Then I held the edge of the glass against my neck, the spot where I had first felt a pulled muscle which turned out to be a tumor, which turned out to be treatable with six months of chemotherapy, except that it didn't work, and so it might not be treatable, and I was finding out if it was tomorrow. Standing among the devastation with the glass against my throat; feeling, from the inside, the warmth of my blood pumping gently along the edge of the shard of glass, which even under a microscope would appear as smooth and clean as the wall of a tsunami. And I slowly scraped the edge of the glass along my skin and, oddly, it reminded me of the way I would slowly slide the edge of my cock along the edge of Nothereal's gorgeous cunt until she screamed. Beauty herself was born of blood and foam. And wouldn't it feel as good as that? And the blood coming out and the tumor will feel as good as that. Finally.

Here I could really, as they say in Hollywood—or at least apparently as film director and Brooklyn native Darren Aronofsky said to Mickey Rourke, which is kind of depressing in a way—try to "bring it," and write that, on the edge of this cliff, skating on the pond at the edge of the wood, at the edge of this broken shard of heavy glass, the buildup met its dialectical payoff, and that for the first time in really how long I saw myself as if in a mirror and there was a rescue. But the truth is that we hysterics and opera lovers depend on a bifocal lens of perception far more than we should: that a more accurate representation of life is less dramatic than the alterity of walls of sound and silence in Mozart, or the fast-slow-fast-slow of the Rolling Stones. Life is more like a series of gradations, a color wheel. What I mean to say is this:

What I realized is this:

(Jeez, writing this is way harder than I thought. Because most of this stuff, you know, I've just been copying from journals I kept when I was sick, but now I'm actually *writing*, and it's harder than you'd think.)

Okay, so the first image I had when I was about to kill myself was that it was just me and a mirror, me standing in front of a mirror, staring mutely at my reflection, and there was no sound and no language and just the blood pumping. But then—

This is what's hard to describe, but I realized that that wasn't the case at all. Rather, it was me *between* two mirrors, producing an infinite line of selves, like at the end of *Citizen Kane*, when Orson Welles walks between the two mirrors—except in a good way.

"Good," in that these many selves, logically then, *must* take up exactly as many different positions in space—virtual positions, perhaps, in that the whole thing was in a way an illusion produced by mirrors, but different positions nonetheless.

So that:*

How do we position suffering in human life? This was the

---

* Look it up! Hint: *Cantos!* Not too far in! Go for it!

crucial question. It *is* one position, suffering. But it's not the only position. It is one position at a specific point in time and space. But human beings are more than that; they do not exist at only one position at a specific point in time and space. Human beings are all over the place and whenevertime. It's an odd fact, and perhaps you will find this idea juvenile; but to me, in that moment, it was important—if only in the sense that if I hadn't had this realization, then you would not be reading these words, because I would have dug that shard of glass so nice and deep, tracing out where the tumor had been, and then you would not be reading these words because I would have collapsed and bled to death. But now I always had, *via* music, a sensitivity to form, where one is in relation—I already said this, I think, at the beginning—one feels a relationship to a frame, which could be a physical surrounding like where you're sitting in a Starbucks, or where you are on an island in Greece or on an island at the mouth of the Hudson River; and the same could be said for time, you might be on the edge of a night or the edge of a morning, or indeed on the edge of the sunset where afternoon turns into morning.

I'm so glad I realized this, because I did *not* enjoy not having been born. But perhaps this wasn't entirely some screenwriter's *deus ex machina*, some sort of divine intervention. The ironic moral to this story may well be that tucked away within and behind my madness was, in fact, the very "humanistic," old-school, unfashionable literary education bestowed on me via my parents, all that reading I'd done which I'd felt so guilty about and which on some level (again, the morphine delusion) I felt had somehow put me in the hospital, and for which on some level I'm afraid you, reader, will hate me, just like that girl who read some of this and then never talked to me again—it may have actually been a saving grace. Because let's go back to that description Mr. Tytell gives of Pound's breakdown in the gorilla cage. There was more to it—I saved the rest for now. Let's rewind just a second, and then continue. No, too far. Stop. No, go ahead. Goddammit, gimme the remote. Okay. Now.

> Pound, the man of words, was now caught in the most overwhelming moment of his life without the power to summon language.[21]

But here's what's next.

> But he might have realized, in some silent corner of his being, that language was merely the artistic fiction of tragedy, the rationalization of pain, and that the flow of words would be invented by the novelist or playwright, or Pound himself in the *Cantos* he would soon begin to write, to stylize and heighten and explain the conjunction of superior forces and the puny human who could dare to defy them.[22]

Well and so that's the thing: I literally—well not *literally*, my dad always complained my mom misused that word, like this one time they were supposed to have dinner with friends, a married couple, and he was working late at the office writing advertising copy he despised and he just couldn't get out of it and so basically he stood her up like Ray Liotta did to Lorraine Bracco in *Goodfellas* (which is how the characters fell in love, not unincidentally) and she told him afterward, "I was *literally* a third wheel." Well no you're not literally a wheel, you're more than a wheel for heaven's sake, you're my wife. Obviously he didn't say that to her—he told me after. And then he talked about the misuse of the word "ironically" in NFL sportscasting. (I don't have time to get into this here, I've gotta go meet a friend of mine, but—if you're from Wisconsin, you're pretty much fascinated by football by default, no matter what. And even me—the only sport I really understand and love is tennis, but still, football—let me put it this way. My father, after a stroke slash maybe nervous breakdown slash losing a lot of money in the crash of Black Monday 1987 slash his son realizing that literature could potentially be of some worth somehow somewhere at some time—he gave up all his belongings [not really] and wandered to the desert like a Christian ascetic [really! kinda] and roomed with me for a while in Chicago and Franzen came over [actually really!] and then moved to Los Angeles [definitely really!] and died [definitely]. And we went over there, my brother and I, and, just like what they said about Orson Welles who died at his typewriter, what better way to go, there was a real typewriter in the apartment with a real unfinished poem in there, which I will not reprint [but I will reprint a few other things, just you wait], and there were piles of manuscripts and piles of books but there was nothing on the walls except for a huge poster of Brett Favre. Piles of books and stuff in different languages but nothing on the walls except for Brett Favre. So that should tell you something. And my father as a tennis player was on the pro circuit as a youth. [But he'd satirize the NFL sportscasters: "Down at three and *ironically*, that's exactly where the quarterback of the Jets last week" and he'd get pissed off—*that's not irony*. But he came not only from literature but from radio and TV so he'd know, standards were higher then.])

So I can't use "literally." But I guess I can use the whole idea of the *literary* in some self-saving sense—if only in the sense that I saw manifold but ordered reflections of myself, each endowed with a different hue of self-awareness: and, most important, that this self-awareness, just as Pound "might have realized," is in the form of a flow of words not yet invented—the flow of words that has just been invented here, now. The many reflections were, in fact, many selves: one that lost itself in the tight and soft sublimity of Nothereal's body; one that saw the line back to the child in my parents' book on Klee; one that was bidding good-bye to the body and the mind the morning of its almost death; and there were also selves infused with other selves: one that saw Caroline watching herself crack a whip in front of a client and thinking this is absurd; one that saw Sophie deftly performing the tightrope walker's walk of playing the role of a woman in New York whose mind was actually at ease; one that saw Nothereal, easily the most opaque example here, aware of her condition on one level and, on another, its helpless victim, like a nation of people can be rendered a victim, rendering her a victimizer, like a nation of people can be rendered a victimizer.

So the intelligently underemphatic ending, the certainly not disappointing truth: that moment in my apartment with the glass at my throat was not as hysterically climactic as I might like to believe now or, indeed, perhaps wanted to believe then. But I did breathe some kind of sigh of relief, as if something like a chapter had ended (and indeed I think it had) (notwithstanding a few aftershocks). I put the glass down, and I called my mom. I remember, while dialing her number, thinking about those books called *Fifty Things To Do before You Die*, or whatever, and how bullshit they were because there's only one thing to do before you die, and that's not die. I'd turned down my mom's offer to fly in from Milwaukee to accompany me at my appointment for the scan results. I told her I'd changed my mind; would she be willing to fly in? Sure, she said. Great, I said. Thanks a lot. Then I called the suicide hotline and gave a brief description of the events of the evening, and a very nice gentleman calmed me down. I collapsed on my bed and fell into a deep sleep for about four hours. I awoke when my mom knocked at the door. I let her in. She was totally cool about the carnage; I said I'd been upset by comments made by a woman I'd been involved with, and that I was worried about the results of the scan—all entirely normal. I made some coffee, we cleaned up the place, went over to the hospital. Scan looks fine, the doc said. I made an appointment with a shrink, and my mom and I had lunch at Da Silvano and then caught *The French Connection* at the Film Forum. We sat in the first row. I gauged the audience's reaction, as I tend to do now, watching the film and watching the watching. As good as the film is, the car chase has been rendered less effective due to its familiarity; but Hackman's performance still startles.

·

ARE WE TALKING about suicide? No. I never wanted to kill the self; I wanted to kill the disease. Suicide, I think, is something else. Pound got away, for instance, but Hemingway didn't. That's a bit odd, isn't it? Given everything. And now everything lately. David Foster Wallace, September 12, 2008. Our greatest writer. As if I wasn't thinking of him during that whole thing. My God. As if he hadn't helped. Not just the writing but the human being. And I know but then Rachel Wetzsteon. As if I wasn't thinking of her thinking about Auden. I mean that's the whole thing and I never even got a chance to ask her. Not my fault but still. Christmas 2009. And this whole thing's about Auden, in that sense—it's not about Pound. It's about Auden and Rachel. And Alexander McQueen—February 2010. What the hell? And for that matter if we're speaking of the fashion world—unfairly criticized from the outside by the feminists who may well paradoxically long for the reappropriation of the aesthetic, of which the object of their scorn is the sole and lonely survivor, Pound and his pre-Raphaelites long since gone—the model Daul Kim? Her unforgettable face—the Korean and the Tartan and the Hun? It's one thing to give it up and move to Jersey or Los

Angeles or (okay, if you're extremely lucky) to Milwaukee. But suicide? And another model, Ruslana Korshunova, at the age of twenty flinging herself off a high-rise three blocks from where I'm sitting, right now, writing? (Too big a word, "writing." Frapping.) Remember it wasn't so long ago that a woman of Ruslana's beauty gave birth, in a bloody foaming, to Western literature, of which we are presently a part. Helepolis, destroyer of cities! Heliandros, destroyer of men! Remember that not so long ago that a woman of Ruslana's beauty sat back and watched the world destroy itself over her. (Or maybe she didn't sit back but, as Pound's ex-girlfriend H.D. felt, she felt terrible, and took herself out of the picture and moved to Egypt to wait the whole thing out. If so, she's still there.) For Pound, the essential tragedy was that "poor old Homer" was blinded by Helen's beauty, and thereby "transmitted it for all ages even though he never saw it with his own eyes but only 'echoes it' in the terrified chatter of old men." In other words, the tragedy wasn't a question of Eve's teeth sinking into the flesh of the apple: the tragedy was that Adam, blinded by her beauty, never saw it with his own eyes, and terrified, has chattered madly about her ever since.[23] But press "ahead" a few

times on the remote and somehow Ruslana, far from blinding our first and only author with her beauty, far from destroying the world, herself is destroyed, at the age of twenty, by the world; she somehow manages to let herself drop off the sheer side of a high-rise, unseen. That's not water down there, that's concrete. And Mr. McQueen, and Ms. Wetzsteon, and Mr. Wallace. I did *not* enjoy not having been born, and perhaps it wasn't entirely some screenwriter's *deus ex machina*, some sort of divine intervention, and my goodness I do love being alive, sitting here with this first edition of the *Cantos* my father gave me—and maybe, you may well argue, the house is too thick and the paintings a shade too oiled (and the old voice lifts itself, weaving an endless sentence), and you may well be right—but my goodness, fuck you, I happen to be so happy to be here with all these gifts and words and all these selves. And here this text was intended as a riposte to the literature of disease, so many of those books I read at the beginning of the whole thing and none of them any help, pure dreck, pale pastel book after book on the shelves in the chains that probably sell scented candles not just to increase revenue but to mask the smell of paper: pale pastel book after book, each one the same, the three-act structure of (I) diagnosis, and (II) the discovery of how beautiful life actually is and how there's more to it than my hedge fund job ever told me it was and look at how lovely this flower is and this butterfly and this herbal tea, and (III) recovery and a book deal and getting a little place in Vermont maybe. If there are some who require disease to teach them such things then fine, but I am not, was not, one of those, thank you very much. I loved life and found beauty and sources of pleasure in things on the outside and on the inside, and illness was not an opportunity for existential awakenings, it was the very opposite of beauty or grace, it was a harrowing, a *descensus*: and then went down. The principle emotions were terror and above all rage. But never a death wish. And then I suppose I have to grudgingly admit that there may be something about coming out on the other side—like the morning I woke up and impulsively grabbed a bottle of Evian and drank, and it was the first time in months that I could swallow. Or not too long after that, when I could swallow food. It didn't matter that I threw it up immediately, just the fact that I could swallow food. And then, not too long after that, walking outside, alone, in the air, two blocks through the bright mist to my café, where I walked indoors, ordered a coffee, and, trembling, took it outside and sat down at the cheap little table with my notebook, like a normal person, and an old man, walking slowly by, warmly remarked, "Now that's the life." (He was right.) Those two blocks that morning were a voyage to Cythera, an epic journey to an island, myrtle green, and back. And the rediscovery of taste: salt came back first (my favorite), then the rest. So yes there is a rebirth and I'm not saying the whole thing was worth it but of course, to be alive again, to at least not be probably dying in this present moment for two years, to have reacquired the resources of the senses and just the pleasures provided by perception, all of this regained: of course there is some sort of renewal. Orson Welles famously said that RKO gave him "the greatest train set a boy could ever play with," and this has been misinterpreted. He wasn't talking about the resources of a Hollywood studio: he was talking about the resources of life. Maybe he didn't know it, but still.

So I don't think my story is about suicide. I don't know how close I was that night. I don't think it was very close. I really don't think I *wouldn't* have realized—*realized*, not remembered,

because I obviously knew the fact but for some reason I hadn't ever really felt it until then—the thing about the multiplicity of selves and thus the thing about the suffering self is merely one of these selves. So my story is not these other stories—Mr. McQueen, and Ms. Wetzsteon, and Mr. Wallace, and Ms. Kim, and Ms. Korshunova—these five people, muses and musers, who basically occupied themselves with showing us beauty (I don't mean to be reductive; for Mr. Wallace, art existed to "disturb the comfortable and comfort the disturbed"; and echoing this, Mr. McQueen, whose design vocabulary extended to "showers of live moths; amputees; walking on water; a woman reclining in a vast glass box, almost swallowed up by her rolls of fat and naked apart from her elaborate breathing apparatus; the model Shalom Harlow being spray-painted by a machine in Jackson Pollock style," once remarked, simply, "I try to protect people"[24]), these five people who disappeared within the span of 517 days. That's about one every hundred days. Aren't these precisely the people who should not disappear? Should this concern us? When I learned of Mr. Wallace's death my first thought was very like that voiced by the literary critic Michael Silverblatt on his radio program *Bookworm* a few days later: "Has something further happened in the world that makes it harder for a sensitive and intelligent person to want to stay alive? . . . The death of David Foster Wallace seems to speak to the difficulty of life itself. Depressed or not, brilliant or not, are we living in a time that makes it hard for us to find the things that allow us to want to stay alive?"[25] What happens when you can't find the train set? In other words, we probably should not stop ourselves from wondering whether, as we continue to move ahead, we should move with a little caution, and make sure that we keep enough room for two mirrors: for one is evidently not enough.

Ruslana Korshunova.

VIII

GUTENBERG'S FOLLY

I am not sentimental.

— *Vanessa Duriès*, Le Lien

This is much later, now, of course. I'm in New Hampshire, beautiful lake country. It was an impulse decision to come up here from the Cape. I can think clearly up here; the city can be intellectually claustrophobic, what with the low-ceilinged apartments, the earsplitting noise and lack of sky. It's early morning: I'm sitting on a lake, paging through a book I still haven't read, my father's copy of Saint Augustine's *Confessions*.

So what happened?

I actually like lakes more than oceans, anyway, having grown up on a lake myself; the blue is more pungent, and they're smooth, smooth enough to allow a small pool of petrol to spread unperturbed, amply, into a black and gold plate, shimmering like an insect's wing, radiating, really approaching insubstantiality, like the Euclidean plane that bisects space. I remember taking a motorboat out on a lake in upstate Wisconsin with my father when I was young. The smell of petrol on a predawn lake, while environmentally harmful, is nevertheless one of the most beautiful odors in the world.

The scan was clear, and my mom and I went to see *The French Connection* at the Film Forum; we sat in the front row. Here's what happened: our hero, an NYPD cop named "Popeye" Doyle, played by Gene Hackman, has clumsily stumbled onto one of the largest smuggling schemes in history. He's set up a trap for the villain, the French smuggling mastermind Alain Charnier (beautifully played by one of Buñuel's favorite actors, Fernando Rey). Charnier and the other buyers and sellers meet in a warehouse, and the deal is sealed, smoothly. They don't realize they're surrounded by Popeye and a contingent of narcotics officers until it's too late. A tightly drawn cat-and-mouse game ensues in the warehouse, played out in silence, not unlike the end of *The Third Man*. I wonder if William Friedkin, the director, had this in mind. (My father's two favorite movies were *The French Connection* and *The Third Man*. He liked thrillers. He didn't quite come around to the notion of film as "high art," or whatever, until quite late; and then, only sporadically.) Popeye sees Charnier and fires—but it's not Charnier. It's the FBI agent who'd also been working on the case, and whom Popeye despised. Popeye's partner, "Cloudy" Russo (the superb Roy Scheider), is aghast: but Popeye is unperturbed. He walks off, as if in a trance: he disappears from (our) view; he's in a different moral universe now. There's the sound of a single gunshot. The film ends. We don't know who fired the shot, nor who received it. It's one of those intelligently underemphatic endings, not some hysterical climax. It's realistic. Of course then again it should be—it's based on a true story. And title cards, in silence, before the end credits begin, let us know what happened after that.

The villain, Charnier, was never caught. He somehow escaped to France.

Carmilla never did chemo, nor radiation, much to the distress of her oncologists; her tumor disappeared; she moved to Minneapolis for a while, then came back to the city, where she is now, still partying, still healthy, still radiant.

Charnier's shady lawyer, Weinstock, was arrested, tried, and released without spending even a day in prison.

Caroline successfully completed rehab and moved back home to start a new life—a life in which stripping and dancing and whipping and all sorts of other activities are performed at her behest, not at the wills of others.

Charnier's mobster partner, Sal Boca, was arrested, tried, and released with the lightest of penalties.

Sophie's alive and well and living in New Jersey.

The NYPD transferred both Popeye and Cloudy out of narcotics.

Nothereal fled in despair to Greece. Funny how in times of crisis we Europeans still try to get back to Greece. She sent me a very sad letter. She was hoping against hope that one day I would forgive her, but she knew I could never forgive her. She was from Serbia: I had squeezed her hand on a hill of domes, overlooking a winter cityscape, in a dream: my hospital room, like my apartment with its carpeting of shards of wood and glass, was a kind of laboratory, with much apparatus: like Klee in his analysis of various perversities, she brought the medical and the experimental to the fore. On February 24, 2009, the *New York Times* ingratiatingly reported "the Association of American Colleges and Universities recently issued a report arguing the humanities should abandon the 'old Ivory Tower view of liberal education' and instead emphasize its practical and economic value." There is science: for example, the complex medical science of pain management, which is employed by a doctor to help a patient; but what if the doctor is also unknowingly a patient, without a doctor? Then the vehicle might veer off the highway, and orange cones will have to be brought out; then harm can occur, not necessarily intended or unintended but maybe as the result of an experiment or accident. Experiments and accidents showed us that mustard gas could both kill tumors and flay the skin off soldiers' backs like when, in Ancient Greece, Apollo peeled Marsyas's skin off his body and nailed it to a tree; experiments and accidents showed us that uranium, that most silvery of elements, could be used to both ionize atoms of the DNA of a harmful cell, leaving healthy cells behind and vaporize entire human bodies, leaving behind shadows of carbon on concrete.

Chicago-born William Friedkin's movie *The French Connection* won the 1971 Academy Award for Best Picture, and he went on to direct *The Exorcist*, which is a story about God and vomiting.

In a way, I went on to write a story about God and vomiting.

•

I MISS MY father; he died, as I mentioned, in 2001, and that sad event was swiftly followed by terrifying suicide attacks—one morning a pair of hijacked commercial airplanes split two skyscrapers that stood six blocks away from my apartment nearly in half, and later that day they collapsed into dust. (I remember those buildings so well, from my first trip to New York; I remember them with tactile memory: I'd placed my hands against one of them and looked straight up

Master of Osservanza, *Burial of Saint Monica and Saint Augustine Departing from Africa*, c. 1430.

against the absolutely sheer, fourteen-hundred-foot-tall façade that really approached a Euclidean plane in air.) And this catastrophe was succeeded by the emotional collapse of my mom, a frightening diagnosis, medical treatment that failed, a considerably dimmer outlook on survival, a second (and highly debilitating) treatment that carried its own mortality rate, medical bills approaching a million dollars, the death of a friend, a nervous breakdown, the death of another friend.

I group these unfortunate events together into an eight- or nine-year chapter. Saint Augustine (whom Pound, shamefully, called the "drunken African"[26]) writes of "nearly nine years" that "passed in which I wallowed in the slime of that deep pit and the darkness of falsehood." I'm reading my father's copy that he bought in 1941, and at this phrase, in the margin, he'd written, "mine is 8 so far." I don't know when he wrote that.

I'm sitting at the side of this lake, paging through this book. On page 345, we have Saint Augustine looking forward to "that pre-eminent rest, when our soul shall have passed through the waters which have no substance." Next to this my father scrawled

! ?

Elsewhere, Saint Augustine is talking about his son. "There is a book of ours," he writes, "which is entitled *The Master*. It is a dialogue between him and me." My father had scrawled an alarmingly tall exclamation point next to this passage, and written in way of explanation, "This is shocking! My book is a dialogue between my son & me! Augustine did it too!" I wonder what book this is. It's somewhere, within the tens of thousands of typewritten pages and handwritten manuscripts that, after his death, were, oddly enough, still there. So my brother and I gathered them together, in Wisconsin, near a lake; divided them in two, and split them up between New York and Los Angeles, at two oceans.

This is a great book, the *Confessions*. I never did read enough, can't even go into that, I wasted my time learning about music, although it might not have been as indulgent a waste as I'd feared. But listen to this: Chapter XII of Book Twelfth of the *Confessions* is entitled:

Of the intellectual heaven and formless earth, out of which on another day the firmament was formed.[27]

Next to this, my father writes, "magical." I wonder what he thought was magical here.

I suspect it was the phrase "on another day." In fact, I'd bet on it.

True story: Saint Augustine and his mother, Monica, had intended to sail from Rome to Africa, but she died before they could make the trip. Days before she died, they were standing at a window that looked down upon a courtyard. The courtyard enclosed a garden. They both experienced a sudden glimpse of eternity, which suddenly vanished.

Saint Augustine was born in Algeria. I googled "Saint Augustine" and two websites caught my attention. In one, a Muslim writes, "St. Augustine was before Islam and here utters words that speak well to us as Muslims."[28] In the other, an American writes, "More disgusting behavior from Islamic thugs."[29] But enough about poor Saint Augustine—we're running out of time, and pages, and I want to talk about my father a bit before we finish up. He was a gifted writer but he never published. Kafka admitted somewhere that anything he wrote was "perfect," by which he meant, he explained, that there was "style" already imbued in whatever came out of his pen. My father once said a similar thing about his own writing. I can't recall exactly how he put it, but it was startling to hear, because he was a modest man. "You certainly don't have to pursue the arts," he said once, "but you certainly can." Maybe that's why I wrote music instead of words—writing music isn't really writing, it's designing. And another startling admission he made was when he said that, while Kafka was his favorite writer, he couldn't stand the fiction, it was only the journals that mattered to him. Which really, now that I mention it, helps us round out the curve here—the motif of journals and memoirs.

When I was in high school and fell in love with a girl for the first time, and fell out of love with science and fell in love with literature and all that artsy stuff I had hated before, my father had something between a nervous breakdown and a midlife crisis. That might have been a coincidence, but as I discovered literature, he rediscovered literature through his son, and that's why I'd like to have a child someday. (I say that now! And all my friends warn me—rethink. It's a lot of work. But still. Plus they're so cute. That's what you think. But they are. And in the end we agree.) I took a trip to New York with this high school girl—in those days, and from Milwaukee, New York was a big deal, a big city, you were on an airplane and you were flying into this huge city, and the plane dipped and you could see the

Empire State Building like a little model, casting a shadow from the orange setting sun: and back then New York actually was a big city, because you could go to the Gotham Book Mart on Forty-Sixth Street: you could walk in, it was really there. I mean you could literally get on an airplane in Milwaukee and fly through the air and wait and then see Manhattan below you, and you could try to see, as you were landing, and as the plane tipped, if you could identify Forty-Sixth Street; and you could grab your girlfriend's hand and you could be in love and be flying into Manhattan.* Readers my age and slightly older than me will know what I'm talking about, and readers younger (sadly, legion) might not, but let me put it this way: the Gotham Book Mart was where wise men fished, if there wasn't a freshwater lake around, predawn, smooth. And it was there that I bought my father a copy of the facsimile of Eliot's original draft, with Pound's annotations, of *The Waste Land*—I love facsimiles, as you by now know—and even though it had been

---

* I mean you can look it up online, but this was the kind of bookshop where the owner started a James Joyce society and the first guy to join was T. S. Eliot. And the comedian Woody Allen said that the Gotham Book Mart was "everyone's fantasy of what the ideal bookshop is." And if the store had once safeguarded and distributed banned books by Arthur Miller and Anaïs Nin, and if your girlfriend is somewhat intrigued by Anaïs Nin, and if you're both so young (too young, was the problem partly, what on earth can one do about that?) and enjoying conversations and flying into Manhattan, and if the Gotham Book Mart is a few thousand feet below, and if you're holding her laughterloving hand, and she's wearing black knit stockings, then you might understand why Woody Allen uses the words "fantasy" and "ideal."

published in 1971, he didn't have it. So we flew back to Milwaukee and I gave it to him, thinking he already had it—I couldn't believe he didn't have it, but he didn't have it. So this gave rise to a bunch of interesting conversations that I'm pretty much still having with him.

When my brother and I were children, he'd write us these marvelous stories. Here's part of one of them.

The Adventures of
Little Dee (d) & Kinto

Chapter 22:
Little Dee (d) Misplaces His Tuba

Little Dee (d) has misplaced his tuba, and thus cannot play in the marching band in the football game.

Kinto plays the finger cymbals and has not lost those, so he can play.

However, a marching band without a tuba is no band at all, or not much of one, and so it is essential that Little Dee (d) find his tuba. He has looked everywhere for it and cannot seem to find it. Kinto wonders how Little Dee (d) can lose his tuba. A tuba is a mighty big thing to lose; you'd think if you looked around for it you'd see it somewhere. If you saw it, you'd notice it immediately.

"I don't know," Little Dee (d) said fretfully, irritated at Kinto for chiding him, and also at himself, for losing it, and also at the tuba, for getting lost. "I've looked everywhere for it."

"Are you sure you've looked everywhere?" Kinto said, emphasizing the word everywhere.

"Well, I haven't looked in my underwear," Little Dee (d) said irascibly.

"Have you looked in Siam?" Kinto said, thinking of all the places it might be where Little Dee (d) possibly—indeed, most likely—hadn't looked. Kinto looked thoughtful again.

"I knew you were going to say something as foolish as that," Little Dee (d) said. "I knew you were going to say something as far out as that. That is really far out."

"Siam is far out," Kinto responded, agreeably. "That's why I suggested it. That's why I thought of it. I was trying to think of far off places where you hadn't looked. I thought you would already have looked around here."

"I did look around a little," Little Dee (d) said. "I haven't looked in Siam."

"Well, why don't you look in Siam?" Kinto said.

It would be easy for Little Dee (d) to look in Siam. Little Dee (d) could whee.

Wheeing is the ability to go someplace very fast. It is not to be confused with wheezing, which is what you do when you get an asthma attack, or what you might do after running very hard—say, in a race. Wheezing is the sound of air rushing through the bronchial tubes, when they are constricted. Wheeing does sound a bit like wheezing, though. Anyway, Little Dee (d) can whee, so he could get to Siam and back in time. It wouldn't be any trouble.

"Why don't you whee to Siam and see if your tuba is there?" Kinto said, suggesting Little Dee (d) go to Siam by whee.

"How could my tuba be there if I never took it there?" Little Dee (d) said. "I've never been in Siam."

"I thought you told me you've been everywhere," Kinto said, amazed.

Little Dee (d) was exasperated with the whole thing—the conversation he was having with Kinto, and with Kinto in particular—so he ended it and that was the end of the Siam adventure.

A note to the reader

Chapter 22 is fairly late in the story, so you have some catching up to do.

First of all, who is Little Dee (d), and why is there always this (d) behind his name? And who is Kinto?

Little Dee (d) and Kinto have already been introduced in the story, and yet they haven't been properly introduced. This seems to violate certain canons, of storytelling, for children. First you should introduce your characters.

To each other?

No, not to each other! I assume they have been introduced to each other.

Chapter 23:
The Difficulty Of Fitting Little Dee (d)

Finding clothes to fit Little Dee (d) is difficult, because he is so small. He is less than a quark in size. He is about the size of a subquark, but because a subquark can't be seen (and hence measured), it is hard to know how big Little Dee (d) is or his dimensions. So it's hard to find clothes for him. It's hard to find him. Therefore Little Dee (d) is allowed to run around in his altogether. Or it is thought he does.

A quark is so small it can hardly be seen with the most powerful microscope—one so powerful that your eye, seen from the other way, looks like the sky—and a subquark is smaller than that! A subquark is so small it can only be theorized. And Little Dee (d) was smaller than that!

Nevertheless, Little Dee (d) existed. Of course, he was difficult to find. Difficult to see. There was no point in looking for him, since you couldn't see him anyway.

Relative to Little Dee (d), Kinto was quite large. But of course, anything would be. (Relative to Little Dee (d), even a subquark was large.)

However, Little Dee (d) packs a wallop. Just ask Kinto.

Little Dee (d) lived with Kinto, and that was why he always returned to Kinto. No matter how bad Kinto was—how stupid, how bumbling, how dull—he was loyal, and most of all, he was a known quantity, and, most of all, safe. Kinto was home. Little Dee (d) may not have had anything else, but at least he had Kinto, & that was something.

Little Dee (d) observed that there were many people in the world. He & Kinto were just two. There was no need for them—Little Dee (d) observed that; there were plenty of people (if that was what was wanted), and plenty to do whatever there was to be done. So there was no real need for them at all. Nevertheless, they existed, and so they had to make do as best they could, carving out a life for themselves, and such pleasures as they could find, or create, within that life; and trying to stay out of trouble.

Little Dee (d) liked to make trouble now & then, deliberately. Kinto made trouble accidentally.

SO YOU CAN see how fun it was for my brother and me to grow up with my parents in that house that used to be on a farm owned by a brewer named Pabst; and my mom would sometimes become exasperated with my father, and it was still fun.

My father would write for fun. He had other jobs. I gave him the *Waste Land* book in 1992, and then I finished high school, and went to college, and his marriage dissolved; and he moved to the desert, and I moved to Paris, and then I came back and he died. My brother and I went through the stuff, and one interesting thing we found (among the stuff that we had time to go through, there's tens of thousands of pages) is this, a very funny little thing he put together when I'd given him the *Waste Land* book. It's basically a folder in which he filed junk mail, but he added commentary—so obviously it's a parody of Eliot, as can be seen from the cover, with Wyndham Lewis's famous portrait of the poet framed in the tacky notebook window. Old Possum does not look happy, that's for sure.

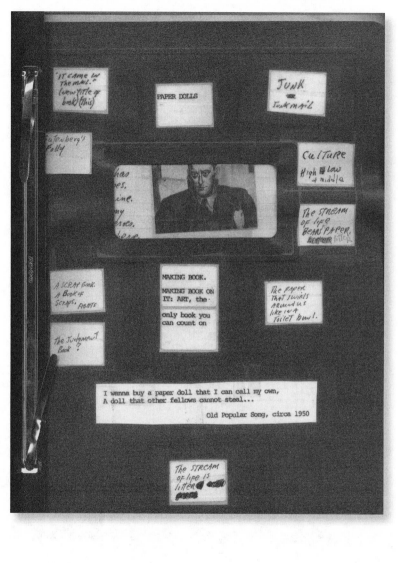

"IT CAME IN THE MAIL." (new title of book) (this)

PAPER DOLLS

JUNK = Junk mail

Gutenberg's Folly

CULTURE High & Low + middle

The STREAM OF life BEARS PAPER.

A SCRAP book. A Book of SCRAPS. FIGHTS

MAKING BOOK. MAKING BOOK ON IT: ART, the only book you can count on

The PAPER THAT swirls around us like in a toilet bowl.

The Judgment Book?

I wanna buy a paper doll that I can call my own,
A doll that other fellows cannot steal...

                    Old Popular Song, circa 1950

The STREAM of life is litter...

The thing begins with almost random jottings—is talk cheap?

limp fingers → Americans are afraid to do a stiff-palm for fear of Hitler,

← who's this?

this face we know. it's President Bush. we all know the face of the President, thru the media

UPI/BETTMANN

"... and will, to the best of my ability, preserve, protect, and defend the Constitution of the United States."

— George Bush
Inauguration Day
January 23, 1989

i can't imagine anything more absurd than a picture of the President in my book.

TALK IS CHEAP.

Is TALK cheap?

I am not a Shaw fan:

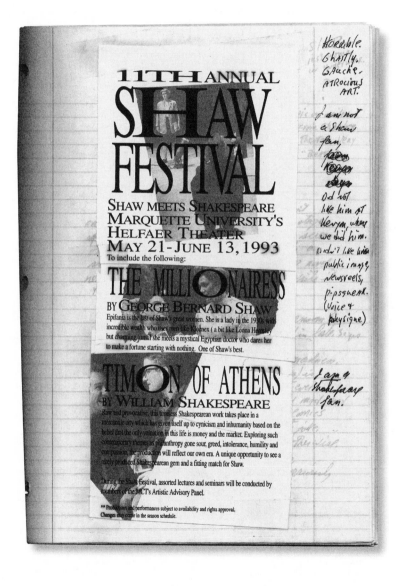

It goes on in this lighthearted vein for about a dozen or so pages, and then the tone begins to change. Notes on Shelley's madness; notes on the linkage between writing and guilt, between writing and obscenity (that Byron, "too, like me, + most good, genuine writers" wrote "dirty").

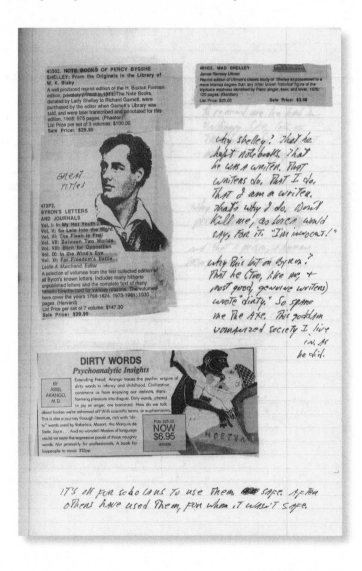

Now: I am not a poet. I is nothing—yet the I remains of interest.

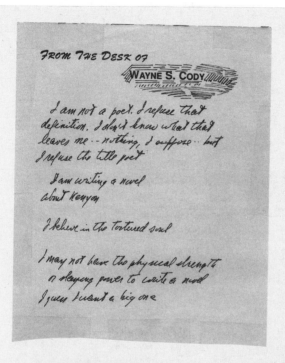

FROM THE DESK OF
WAYNE S. CODY

I am not a poet. I refuse that
definition. I don't know what that
leaves me...nothing, I suppose...but
I refuse the title poet

I am writing a novel
about Kenyon

I believe in the tortured soul

I may not have the physical strength
or staying power to write a novel
I guess I meant a big one

On this business of being a writer. This matter. On this matter of being a writer. There is much talk about it. "I am not — " Auden said that all statements that begin with "I" are false. I should get rid of my "I". It is much too easy to say "I", to begin with "I." I am this or that, or I am not. Sheer egotism. Pure. I is nothing. A big zero. Only as the I relates to, and then one should give only that which it relates to, and cut off the I. Take the I that sees or feels a thing and leave the thing.

Yet the I remains of interest. People are intere ested in one's I. You yourself personally. And to do a he or she, well, that's a dodge, and may not be more interesting for all that, for all that taking the I away. One may be better off with the I after all, the he or she an obvious dodge to escape the stigma of the I. Am I more interesting, to myself, or to others, for being a he or she? That is still me, or I. The attempt to be objective, to see oneself objectively, removing the ½ stigma of narcissism, self-indulgence, self-interest, doesn't work, doesn't fool anybody, least of all oneself.

To think that this whole time I was reading and asking him about literature, everything I read I'd ask him about—I talked to him for weeks about my frustration with Wallace Stevens before he finally admitted he couldn't stand him either, and I was so relieved—and to learn that he'd destroyed a 350-page novel:

> MY 3rd DAY AT THE FAIR
>
> Body builders in muscle shirts. CAliforniA guys. And girls. Blond. (I am sTudying bodies, ThaT being mainly whaT The FAIR HAS To offer, A passing parade of Flesh.
>
> wheelchAiRs.
>
> 3 ENORMOUS WOMEN. EACh is A ball of FAT. MoTher & 2 daughTers. "EAT, Judy, eAT!" So Judy ATe.
>
> SARTRE.
>
> 2 hrs To go.
>
> I burned A 350 pp novel yesTerday. (mine, in ms.) ToDAy A womAn ediTor Asked me for iT.   I'll have To re-wriTe iT. iT wAs A sex novel abouT A womAn who wroTe TrAsh, sofT-core porn RomAnces. I Am going To sleep in This chAir. I wonder If I Am dying? ProbAbly.

There's a lot of midwestern humor in there, but who is this editor, this woman who wanted to see his novel? What novel?

> SCRAPS. Scrap. Fights.
> One must be scrappy. One must scrap.
>
> RESISTING FIGHTING
> So what if I don't pub. & I go the rest
> or get my music played, my symphonies performed.
> I must live with myself, mustn't I? As long as I
> can live with myself I'm alright, it's ok. life.
> One must FIGHT for the arts, what one believes in.
> Why is it necessary to be so (goddamned)
> impudent? (who am I saying this to? my mother.)
> Gods rise from below, the underworld.
> NAMES
> Named after days of the week
> Maunday
> Tuesday   Weld, the day we weld
> Wednesday   Wed-nes-day, the day we wed.
> Thursday   The day we thirst
> Friday   The day we fry
> Saturday   The day we sit, or sat, earlier
> Sunday   The day we sun.
>
> When you are ▮▮▮▮, you get either grief (worship?
> or indifference n jealousy
>
> It is all to God. I am talking to God
> the unseen listener.
>
> what is wrong with staying home &
> perfecting one's art? Practicing practicing!

Interesting that he was reading Rushdie, I wonder which one. And the final page:

> *Should we separate?*
>
> ```
> The wife and I?
> The girlfriend and I?
> The boyfriend and I?
> The world and I?
> My thoughts one from another?
> My hair?
> Cream from milk?
> Milk from cow?
> Cow from herd?
> One color from another?
> I from my friends?
> I from this town?
> I from my emotion(s)?
> ```

Not long after he finished writing this notebook, my parents did separate. I was living in Europe. My brother decided to go to college in Los Angeles. My father asked him if he wanted a ride. Sure, my brother said. So one fall morning they got up early and threw some luggage in the car and climbed in and pulled out of the driveway, and my brother asked my father if he'd said good-bye to our mother, and he didn't respond, and off they drove to California; and my parents never saw one another again. My father lived in various places out West—for a while, in a motel on Route 66; for a time in a really tiny town somewhere called Lodi (not the one in California); for a while on the banks of Lake Powell, a stunning reservoir on the Utah/ Arizona border. The dust was bad for his lungs; he wasn't eating well; he smoked and drank coffee and wrote nonstop. He said he didn't commit himself to writing as a youth because he felt he hadn't accumulated enough experiences; but that by the time he tried to catch up, he had accumulated too much experience. He wrote mainly poetry, but also plays and essays, including an essay on the question of pain, also a theme, obviously, of this thing I've been writing. I only visited him once there. We had a great time, doing nothing, really, but talking. He rarely drank. For some reason he had a good bottle of Riesling sitting there, but he didn't have a corkscrew, so we opened the bottle with the aid of a hammer and an awl. We sipped the wine outside, watching the desert turn itself from a desert in the daytime to a desert in the nighttime.

Was this when I was living in Paris? I guess. I forget the chronology—it gets confusing, because I took a year off from college to go live in Paris, and then I came back to finish college, and it was during part of that year that my dad came back to Chicago and we shared an apartment. Even then, my parents didn't see each other—just ninety miles away. And then I moved back to Paris, so I guess it was then that he moved to Los Angeles, not that it really matters.

There's a story about a famous filmmaker I heard or read somewhere, and I don't know if it's true. He sat his wife and family down and explained to them that he loved them very much, but he also loved film, and if it ever became a conflict, he would have to choose film, and he loved them and therefore wanted them to know that. And my dad would often quote Yeats's quote about the choice between "perfection of the art and perfection of the life." To me, my father was one of the most emotionally well-balanced people I've ever known—not that he didn't have his moods, obviously—but overall he was one of the happiest people I've known. My brother, however, thinks that he was profoundly unhappy because he felt creatively unfulfilled. Certainly the question of whether to publish was on his mind—the strength of this preoccupation, as evident in the notebook which purports to be about junk mail but swiftly turns into a meditation on this subject, was a surprise to me. We didn't spend a lot of time talking about the problem of balancing life and art, whether or not to publish, to submit stuff; whether it's important to publish, to be recognized, et cetera. We spent most of the time talking about actual books. (We talked about philosophy sometimes too, especially when I was flirting with getting seriously into philosophy for a period of time in college that lasted maybe eight months. He was excited intellectually by philosophy but it wouldn't stick, he said; the words had no "weight.")

I had been talking before about the task of properly positioning the self that suffers within the other selves; Klee had wondered if he'd given the proper weight to eroticism in his work, as a whole. I guess one of the things that comes up when I think about my father is, what's the proper position of art within a life?

A lifelong smoker, he acquired emphysema, and this mixed with other ailments that come up with aging. He loved Los Angeles, which might seem paradoxical since he might seem like he was an irascible aesthete, but he really wasn't. Then there were health crises off and on in varying degrees of seriousness, but things always seemed to resolve themselves. But then one day I called him and—for some reason—I transcribed part of the conversation, and it turned out to be the last time we spoke. I've already quoted a part of this but it bears repeating.

[My father:] I'm just sitting on the edges of the ends of life, feeling no pressure to do anything, just the visual beauty of nature without worrying about what's going on inside. The real mystery is in the science and the physics; that's the mystery of life, in my opinion. The DNA and the molecular and the chemistry and the biology is just absolutely extraordinary, the intricacy of it just blows me away; the way it evolved.

[Me:] What about art?

[My father:] Art, I think, is an attempt of man's conscious mind to make his own design, and he tries it in engineering, to see if it will work, and I mean he makes a rocket ship that will fly? Well, what the hell, the katydid does that with one arm tied behind his back and does it with painting and so on, nature is so good at that there's simply no comparison. Ransom* said that there's no reason, there's no way we can improve it,

---

* My dad's referring to the poet John Crowe Ransom, his mentor at Kenyon College. My father went to a couple of different colleges but never finished a degree. Ransom wanted him to stay and finish his degree, but my dad was restless. He told me that in their last conversation, he told Ransom that maybe he'd come back, and asked him if he'd still be there. "Oh, I'll be here," Ransom said, a bit wanly.

except maybe a little with our arts, but I don't know if there's much of an improvement. I mean, the most scoffed-at remark in all of literature, Joyce Killmer's—"I think that I shall never see a poem as lovely as a tree"—is the most profound thing ever said about art, because that is absolutely true. From any point of view, whether interior or exterior. And the thing is all built in. It just happens. You know how hard most of the time we have to work for anything good at all in our stuff, right? Meanwhile nature's just throwing this stuff out.

[Me:] That's a very good approach, it's being intellectually honest, yet . . . It's honest in both ways. Envious, astonished by the whole thing, and yet somewhat skeptical, wondering if it's a virtue or not.

[My father:] I find your writing also often takes some very interesting self-saving turns! (Laughs.)

[Me:] Have you read David Foster Wallace's essay on tennis? He played when he was younger. He said Stefan Edberg's hobby, apparently, is staring at walls.

[My father:] Gee, that's great. He's my kind of guy.

He meant Edberg, not Wallace. He never read Wallace. And funny that he mentioned my "writing," because I hadn't written. I wonder what he was talking about. When we had that conversation I had already bought a ticket for LA, was due to leave in a couple of weeks; a few days later my brother—who was living out there—called and said—hmm, this looks kinda bad. And I said—should I fly out now? And he said—well, wait. And then an hour later my brother called back, and he was gone.

We cleaned up the apartment, pretty much spotless, an oxygen tank, nothing on the walls except for the poster of Favre, and books and reams and reams of paper, poems endlessly redone, hundreds of versions of the same poem (that was his problem, maybe—didn't have the need to finish), and the manuscript in the typewriter, midsentence, paused, like Welles. My brother and I split up the books and the manuscripts and my gift to him—the *Waste Land* facsimile—was returned to me with an inscription on the frontispiece that reads thusly:

This book was given to me by my son Joshua. That is why I value it. Eliot is important to me (and important, not just to me) but more important is this book because it was given to me by my son Joshua, who is more important to me than Eliot.

Eliot is a great poet (I think) but Joshua is a great son and it is greater to have him as a son than to have Eliot, great poet tho' he is.

I don't, in fact, <u>quite</u> know what to make of Eliot—is he genuine or not? Something spurious about him, devious and/or at least elusive, but I have <u>no</u> doubt about my son Joshua, absolutely genuine.

So while my mind goes back & forth on Eliot, it doesn't on Josh; my love for him and his for me is firm and committed.

Eliot has a world of admirers who love him (and hate him) with varying degrees, so that my admiration for him is not special and unique. But no one loves Joshua more than I do. I have a claim on him no one can equal. What a great boy. What a great son. What a great man to be.

Thanks a lot for the book, this Eliot, Joshua. This makes Eliot's value to me, at times uncertain, often fluctuating, more certain, because you gave it to me.

7/92

P.S. I agree with you: Pound took out some good stuff.

He's referring to a few passages we had talked about. He annotated the book, so we have the urtext and Eliot's corrections and Pound's corrections and comments and my dad's comments. "My thoughts in a tangled bunch of heads and tails": Pound took it out but my father wrote "great—exact." Pound excised a Prufrockian parenthetical "Perhaps it does not come to very much" on grounds that it was "Georgian" and my dad wrote, "Why take out just because Georgian?" And in the fourth chapter, the one that Pound radically truncated, we have a section Eliot called "The Death of a Saint Narcissus," but obviously a description of Saint Sebastian:

> *So he became a dancer to God.*
> *Because his flesh was in love with the burning arrows*
> *He danced on the hot sand*
> *Until the arrows came.*
> *As he embraced them his white skin surrendered*
> *itself to the redness of blood, and satisfied him.*

Now is he green, dry and stained
With the shadow in his mouth.[30]

And my father writes in pencil next to this, "an extremely fine poem, extremely erotic." And obviously discovering this beautiful letter to me, after he had died, was very moving, and the letter tells us another thing about positioning: the positioning of art in life.

A very generous thing to do, to write that letter. Since his death, he's appeared in three dreams, all related to my diagnosis. (Jeez, dreams again. Maine-born Carroll Terrell, that late, eminent Ezra Pound/Stephen King scholar, wrote that Yeats's "whole work, early and late, is so filled with dreams that assigning a specific source can only be idle speculation.")[31] When I felt the thing in my neck, I taught my music history class at Columbia and then went over to health services in John Jay Hall, where Lorca had lived when he was the poet in New York. A male nurse checked it out and said don't worry about it, it's just a virus, and for some reason I didn't think so; I asked for a second opinion. So another white coat came in, a woman this time, and said, yeah, you should get that checked out right now, so I went directly across town, to the East Side, where an ear-throat-nose guy stuck a needle right into my neck. (He said, don't worry, it's so tiny it's painless, and he was absolutely right, and that was kind of cool, to know that; Caroline was into needle play and occasionally that would freak me out a little, so it normalized that side of things.) And he said, come back in a week, we'll have the results.

So I knew the room. And the night before the next appointment I had a vivid dream in which I was sitting in the room with my father, and the door was half open, and the doctor guy passed by and glanced in and smiled, and kept going, and I felt a rush of relief: my father and I felt a rush of relief: but then the doctor actually came in and said that the tumor was malignant, and my father broke down in tears, in agony, and that was the worst part of the whole thing, seeing him like that.

And oddly enough the next day, I was sitting in the same room—not with my father, obviously, but with my brother, Matthew—and the door was half open, and I knew what was going to happen. And I kid you not—the doctor guy passed by and glanced in and smiled, and kept going, and then I knew what the deal was. It was the dream, exactly: played out on my retina, like a dream. And then the doctor really did come in and say that the tumor was malignant, and my brother and I, stunned, took a weird walk through Central Park, silent.

I told Matthew about the dream. It meant that I was dying. Obviously my father knew I was going to die, and that's why he cried in the dream.

Matthew: "No, no, I don't think so." (Matthew knows much more about dreams, and Jung, and really everything, than I do.) The dream, obviously a vision, meant that I would survive; the tears of the father were tears of joy: that I, a writer, needed to feel terrific pain before releasing my subject, but that I would release my subject: that I was transforming from the "man to be" to a "man": that I was assuming his place.

In retrospect, those words from my brother formed the first

ray of hope. In the second dream, after I had started chemo, I was having a conversation with my father, we were strolling somewhere, I think in Central Park (in film, this is called a "walk and talk"). I can't remember the subject of our conversation, but his body parts were disappearing, one by one, and neither of us made any reference to that fact.

The third occurred after I learned the chemo didn't work, before the transplant. This really seemed like a visitation: it was obvious that my father was in the underworld: here I was Ulysses, speaking with Achilles. We were making small talk, avoiding the elephant in the room: the fact that my father was dead.

Finally I asked him, so what was death like, anyway? He averted his eyes: my query was a *faux pas*, a breach of some metaphysical protocol.

But I knew him better than that. Come on, I said. What was it like?

He paused, then answered. "Fiery," he allowed. "But totally unlike what you would imagine. And actually, not so bad."

I haven't talked with him since.

IX

THE AGE OF INNOCENCE

And there is no new thing in all this place.
—*Ezra Pound*, "The Tomb at Akr Çaar"

Now the Eskimos have all those words for snow, and David Foster Wallace once said that we should have many more words for gradations of self-consciousness; the Ancient Greeks had several words for love. What I described above—the love between parent and child—they called στοργή, or *storgē*. Romantic or erotic love, another theme of this little essay, they called ἔρως, or *érōs*—a whole different thing. And there's a question the extent to which their concept of ἔρως is isomorphic with our notion of romantic love, but for our purposes, just for right now, sitting beside this lake, it'll suffice, since the other thing that occurs to me when I think about all this stuff and, inevitably, about Carmilla and Caroline and Sophie and Nothereal is how absurdly far any of this stuff is from "love"—romantic love. When both parties understand this, the resulting intimacy creates its own sort of love, I suppose: the shared love of Love, an object each party regards from a certain distance, each party then bound to the other in the very absence of the object: here the director of photography would want to shoot the lovers' faces not facing each other, but spooning, both looking off in the same direction, through the salty Mediterranean sea mist that stings their eyes, periwinkle after the sun's setting—or later, because we're over schedule, the leading actress just suffered another nervous breakdown, she's locked herself in her trailer, and we've "lost the light"; so everyone waits until it's pitch black, the actress feels better, and now the director has the lovers stand at the helm of the ship or ferry, and the island has already announced itself not through its own form, as was expected in daylight, but, unexpectedly, by blocking out the stars. Of course the writer and the director and the crew and the performers will "work this in" to the story, they might have to reshape a few things here and there, but it's no big deal in the end, and as a matter of fact the original version is, by the time of the wrap party (with champagne glasses tinkling and dresses like in Fitzgerald), entirely forgotten by everyone involved; and the audience, at the premiere three hours ago, never knew another version had been originally intended, and would never know. Remember that the only reason Eliot saved his original manuscript of *The Waste Land* in the first place—he gave it to John Quinn, a lawyer, his patron, and it was lost for years before turning up in the New York Public Library—was that "it is the only evidence of the difference which [Pound's] criticism has made to the poem."[32] Oh and the lovers never get to the island but float past it.

During a crisis of (what do they call it?—yes) "existential" proportions when one is simply not sure if one will be alive in a few months the real thing—by which I mean, I hesitate to say, love, I mean the real thing, I think we all know what that is, of course it's a cultural construct and we can discuss Eleanor's court all we want and twelfth-century Provence all we want and *l'amour courtois* all we want, but we may as well also discuss particle physics then, we may as well discuss cells and atoms then, we know the sharp intake of breath that accompanies the thrill and the swell that, as the serpent opens its mouth, is unlike any other swell or thrill, unyielding, we know when every cell of the body is slightly misshapen, slightly oblong rather than round, so pointed the anticipation, so acute the focus upon the beloved. The wind of that, the grains of sand of that, the angle of the shaft of sunlight of that, the motion of the dust particles illuminated by the shaft of sunlight of that. The Klee colors of that, the yellow spot of Picasso of that. The sheer hurtling forth: the leap, the tipping downward. It's chemical and physiological, and it's stressful; so maybe the body, hunched down in the trenches of survival mode, won't allow the direct experience of love, and settles for the substitute I've described above, a little or a lot like Windows running in safe mode.

Or of course maybe I'm simply incapable of love, with or without the stress of a life-threatening disease.

It's not the *Annie Hall* slash Groucho Marx gag about not wanting to belong to a club that would have me as a member. That's just egoism: nothing's good enough. No, it's more interesting than that. This is the thought that tends to haunt me, flutteringly, raising dust through a sunbeam in some attic of the mind—the basement being too damp for dust: what if my ethical principles prohibit me from subjecting the object of my love to—in a word—*me*?

And what if this *me* isn't the *diseased me*, but the *pre-diseased me*?

The title plates, in silence, speak of the eventual destinies of our characters, and then as the end credits roll—and they just began to roll, with the music ("Can you hear the music?" the dying Isolde asks the audience, with not inconsiderable urgency, at the end of the opera) that just started, the music that signals us to stand up and prepare for the walk back from the darkness into the outdoor light that will, just for a moment, blind us—we can't help but wonder whether there'll be a sequel (turned out there was); whether these lives, sundered, will ever crisscross again; whether Popeye will finally track down the heroin smuggler from Marseilles.

At the same time, it's an ending. Funny how in English we speak of "closing" titles in movies, for instance, referring to the end credits. Or in music: that's a great closer. Or "what did the Stones close with"? It's funny because endings are openings: we leave the theater, we go outside, into the bright mist, maybe to an island, myrtle green. The lights come up. We leave the confines of the stage; the angle expands, the view widens. We feel a breeze, or as Da Ponte, Mozart's librettist, would have called it, a zephyr, over the baked earth, the *terra-cotta*, right?

I'm being oblique here—I'm just thinking of two moments that bookend the whole thing, the diagnosis/hospitalization/recovery thing: two moments that in different ways have to do with love.

As far as the first it's a woman I know I care for so deeply, to whom I'm so irresistibly attracted, that at a certain point I wondered why I never—what? Made love to her, obviously, but also lived with her, had a child with her, supported her, sort of partnered up with her as a companion, this is in a way what marriage is, I guess. One answer to that is that the circumstances were never quite right, she was dating somebody when I was single, I was dating somebody when she was single, but my feelings for her, and hers for me, so greatly and obviously outweighed our feelings for our respective rivals that the obstacles would certainly not be credible in the context of a Provençal tale of unrequited love. Another answer is that we're friends, so sleeping together might "ruin a good thing," although honestly I've never understood this idea, so dear to the hearts of screenwriters and sitcom hacks. Never in my life has sex "ruined a good thing." Why would it? Only if, again, I cherish this woman to the extent that I would never want to inflict myself on her. That's not what the sitcom writers mean, and that's not what Groucho Marx meant. But just look at whom I called that afternoon when the pulled muscle in my neck suddenly was potentially something other than a pulled muscle. Talk about an infliction! Look whom I spent that week with, fretting over the pending results of the biopsy? It should be okay, it'll probably be okay, it's some kind of virus, it's probably nothing but it's good to be sure. Look whom I called with the news. I will never forget her words on the phone, just two words, "Oh Josh," a descending minor third (couldn't be otherwise, could never be otherwise, not in Mozart and not in the Rolling Stones), low register, somewhere between *piano* and *pianissimo*, and I detest hearing my name pronounced but these were the two purest words ever addressed to me, unadorned of self, unself-conscious, unstrategic, not "helping," not afraid, not trying to comfort, not reflective, not God what should I say, not why him and not me, not thank God him and not me, not okay so that's what it was there were two possibilities and this is the one that we're dealing with now, not okay we're going to deal with this you and I, not holy shit I'm freaking out, no empathy, no sympathy, no quick recalibration, no impressive recovery, no rapid inventory, no recontextualization of the events of the past few days, no grave understanding, no coming to terms with mortality, no anger, no shock, no pity, no sadness, no fear. What resides there, then, in the absence of all of those moves of the mind untaken, that the audience will never miss? A soft exhalation of communion.

In other words, love. The subject of another book. But to end this one, I should add that I found basically the same thing—in written words, unvocalized—at the end of the whole business (or deal) when the first big CT scan was fine, my mom and I saw *The French Connection*, and for the first time it looked like perhaps I would actually be one of those people who survived. I popped an e-mail to an ex-girlfriend, not just any ex-girlfriend but—well we hadn't communicated in ages, I mean this is going pretty far back (one time we drove across a black bridge together and yellow grain was turning orange) (and one time we flew into Manhattan together and were excited to go to a bookstore) and why we parted—again, really can't go into this but I hope she won't mind if I take the liberty to quote her: she e-mailed back,

> What wonderful wonderful news. I've been thinking a lot recently about your music; we had a very vivid conversation about it, maybe in a dream but it doesn't seem like it.

Needless to say, it takes a certain gift as a writer to be able to get away with repeating an adjective like "wonderful" within the first four words, not have it seem precious. A certain (read pretty immense) gift to do it without a comma, which risks a pretentious grab for "breathlessness"* to attain the truly expressive dactylic meter, which she then just as thoughtlessly (in the highest sense of the word) abandons, after a single tetrameter, in favor of an offhand, free-verse mention of my music, which has nothing at all to do with my recovery except of course that the fact that it has nothing to do with my recovery has everything to do with my recovery; she is saying that all of those things in life that you were unable even to behold from afar are now being placed back in your hands, restored. Not to mention the reference to a dream—maybe a dream but it doesn't seem like it. We were having a conversation in a dream "and," not "but" (that's the only correction I'd make), maybe we weren't in a dream, because the two of us are two people who are unable to see each other since our breakup, and also we're two people who probably live together pretty much constantly, within our dreams and without them. I'm not going to go through the whole message, which, incidentally, is a model of brevity, but here's how it ends:

> Thank you for this message. Thank you so much for going through all that and getting better.

* You know what I mean? It's like Michelle Pfeiffer's frankly god-awful performance in this movie the father of another ex-girlfriend of mine directed, an otherwise sublime adaptation of Edith Wharton's *The Age of Innocence*, where the only way she can play a scene, apparently, is to rush through the door after having raced up six flights of off-camera stairs. But that woman is another story: that's when I was no longer simply dreaming of recovery: that was sad too, and also not only.

This from a woman, first of all, too modest, herself, to write—in spite of the fact that she's the most gifted of all the writers of my generation I've had the pleasure to meet or read; and this from a woman I mistreated, not once not twice, who suffered at my doings and now is thanking me for having dared to dream, first, of my own death, and then daring to dream of recovery. Theroux ("Dreams, by definition, do not come true") is wrong, Picasso ("Everything you can imagine is real") was right. "Was Picasso *smart?*" this same woman asked me once, long ago, before New York, before Italy, before Paris. I knew exactly what she meant. What a gorgeous mind she has, smooth as sanded sandalwood, and her skin like the petal of a white flower: yes, my darling, he was.

X

CANAL STREET

Let us end this book by answering an old question, rather than posing a new one: who stole the *Mona Lisa*?

—*Norman Mailer*, Portrait of Picasso as a Young Man

Okay, um, here's maybe not such a bad way to end this:

So a lot of the aforewritten (that's not a word, but anyway) was inscribed in longhand, in journals, in hospital rooms, or at the side of a lake; in waiting rooms, or in cafés, where people, obviously, sit in different proximities to vertical walls. So I've got this pretty big stack of journals here, which I term "journals" as opposed to notebooks. Notebooks have horizontal lines. Journals are just big blank pages, so you can make up your own lines. As David Byrne once mused, "Notebooks? What good are notebooks? They won't help you survive." He was correct. Journals, on the other hand, just might.

The *Mona Lisa* at the Musée du Louvre, Paris, France, 2005.

(Obviously these aren't the correct definitions of the words "notebook" and "journal." It's just the way I think of them, and I'm a little tired, this book turned out to be a little longer than I thought, and way more work. Plus I'm hungry. Let's just agree that the word "notebook" strongly suggests ruled paper, and classrooms, and after-school afternoons; and "journal" is a broader rubric.)

Anyway it's funny how each of these journals comes to an end, and then there's another one that follows. Like look at this one here, for example. So on the last page, I wrote—I remember this, I remember writing this, I was sitting in that

258

café over on Church Street—I wrote, "A woman just came up. Is that your paper? I hadn't noticed that I'd been sitting next to a copy of the *Times*. Boston won the World Series. 'Boston Sweeps Series.' That's the headline. I almost asked her why on earth—what with all this—why on earth she'd want to read the *Times*? But I gave it to her, of course, without saying anything. She's taken it back to her seat, on the other side of the café, to my right; she's reading it now. Hopefully she's waiting for someone, anticipating a meeting with a friend or a spouse or boyfriend, and she just needs to pass the time. What I mean to say is—I hope to God she's not just actually reading the *Times*, as an activity in itself: hopefully that isn't the only reason she's here, having coffee at four o'clock in the afternoon, sunnier now than before, the day's turned surprisingly warm, I don't even need the coat I brought. Hopefully she's waiting for someone."

It goes on:

> *I have space left in this notebook for about ten more handwritten lines, and after that I'll have to go buy another one, over on Canal Street. No more pages. I'm heading towards the edge of the last page, even as I write. Canal Street, in the seventeenth century, was the northernmost edge of New York. The key to any kind of composition, it occurs to me, is to write against an edge, a frame. Put a frame around something, anything—the frame of cancer, say, around a life—and you've already gotten somewhere, without even willing it: then, as if by magic or by grace, you're waiting for someone, and can read the Times.*

Acknowledgments

The author is indebted to the following, in roughly chronological order.

Patricia Cody
Matthew Cody
Nancy Bush
Ann Volkwein
Cassie Jones
William Breitbart
Barry Crooks
Rick Dickens
Paul Bozymowski
Katherine Lytle
Anne Philpott
Aaron Adams
Juliette Adams
Theodore Boulokous
Heather Keller

Jonathan Dreyfous
Swanna MacNair
Edward Lovett
Erin Lovett
Gabriel Jones
Belzu DuHoinx
Louis Warren
Ildiko Szollosi
Max Karkégi
Fred Lerdahl
Peter Maxwell Langrind

And then of course Bill Clegg, Jill Bialosky, Alison Liss, Alexandra Pringle, and all the inspired, admired persons at W. W. Norton and Bloomsbury, whose continued demonstration that books are, in fact, collaborative never ceases to create a sense of wonder.

Notes

1. Bob Spitz, *The Beatles: The Biography* (Little, Brown, New York, 2005), 641.
2. Louis S. Warren, *Buffalo Bill's America* (Knopf, New York, 2005), 538–540.
3. C. David Heymann, *Ezra Pound: The Last Rower: A Political Profile* (Viking, New York, 1976), 309.
4. Ibid., 53.
5. Ibid.,62.
6. Nicholson Baker, *U and I: A True Story* (Random House, New York, 1991), 19.
7. T. S. Eliot, *The Waste Land: A Facsimile and Transcript of the Original Drafts Including the Annotations of Ezra Pound*, ed. Valerie Eliot (Harcourt Brace Jovanovich, New York, 1971), 67.
8. Hugh Kenner, "Leucothea's Bikini: Mimetic Homage," in Noel Stock, ed., *Ezra Pound: Perspectives: Essays in Honor of His Eightieth Birthday* (Henry Regnery, Chicago, 1965), 39.
9. David Foster Wallace, *A Supposedly Fun Thing I'll Never Do Again: Essays and Arguments* (Little, Brown, New York, 1997), 189.
10. Heymann, *Ezra Pound: The Last Rower*, 118.
11. Ibid., 298.

12. Will Grohmann, *Paul Klee* (Harry N. Abrams, New York, 1967), 94.

13. Alexander Theroux, "Revenge," *Harper's*, October 1982.

14. Mark Stevens and Annalyn Swan, *De Kooning: An American Master* (Knopf, New York, 2004). 628–629.

15. Madonna, *Sex*, ed. Glenn O'Brien (Warner Books, New York, 1992), 12.

16. Heymann, *Ezra Pound: The Last Rower*, 64.

17. John Tytell, *Ezra Pound: The Solitary Volcano* (Doubleday, New York, 1987), 293.

18. Noel Stock, *Ezra Pound: Poet in Exile* (Manchester University Press, Manchester, UK, 1964), 258.

19. Tytell, *Ezra Pound: The Solitary Volcano*, 246.

20. Ibid., 278.

21. Ibid.

22. Ibid.

23. Carroll F. Terrell, *A Companion to the Cantos of Ezra Pound* (University of California Press, Berkeley, 1980), 29.

24. Lisa Armstrong, "Death, S&M, Violence and Religion Were All There on Alexander McQueen's Catwalk," *Times* (London), February 11, 2010.

25. "Politics of Culture: Considering David Foster Wallace," *Bookworm* radio broadcast, KCRW, September 16, 2008.

26. Tytell, *Ezra Pound: The Solitary Volcano*, 247.

27. J. G. Pilkington, trans., *The Confessions of St. Augustine* (Liveright Publishing, New York, 1942, Black and Gold Edition), 314.

28. *Salikah: A Student's Digest* (blog), August 1, 2007, http://salikah .blogspot.com/2007/08/something-of-confession.html.

29. Thomas J. Lucente Jr., "More Disgusting Behavior from Islamic Thugs," *Light of Liberty* (blog), April 2, 2009, http://www.lucente.org/blog/cate gory/religion.

30. Eliot, *Waste Land*, 97.

31. Terrell, *Companion to the Cantos of Ezra Pound*, 372.

32. Heymann, *Ezra Pound: The Last Rower*, 52–53.

Credits

p. 6: Allen-Bradley Clock Tower retrieved from http://commons.wikime dia.org/wiki/File:Allen_Bradley_Clocktower_8208.jpg.

p. 12: 59th Street Bridge (Queensboro Bridge) (1910) courtesy of Library of Congress, Prints and Photographs Division, Detroit Publishing Company Collection.

p. 16: Acropolis retrieved from http://commons.wikimedia.org/wiki/ File:Acropilos_wide_view.jpg.

p. 16: Taj Mahal and the Yamuna River retrieved from http://commons .wikimedia.org/wiki/File:Taj_Majal_y_rio_Yamuna.jpg.

p. 19: United Nations Secretariat Building Façade retrieved from http:// commons.wikimedia.org/wiki/File:UN_Headquarter_Facade_2005-04-29.jpg.

p. 63: Francesco Guarino's *Sant'Agata si copre le ferita* used courtesy of Museo di Capodimonte, Ministero per i Beni e le Attivita Culturali.

p. 70: Jean-Léon Gérôme's *The Slave Market* retrieved from http://commons .wikimedia.org/wiki/File:G%C3%A9r%C3%B4me_Jean-L%C3%A9on_ The_Slave_Market.jpg.

p. 73: Titian's *The Flaying of Marsyas* retrieved from http://commons.wiki media.org/wiki/File:Titian_-_The_Flaying_of_Marsyas.jpg.